THE ASSOCIATION OF ILLUSTRATORS' THIRD ANNUAL 1977-78

Paper Tiger

The Third Annual of the
Association of Illustrators was
designed by Clive Crook,
and John Tennant assisted by
Alexandra Lapote,
Co-ordinating Editor Alan Austin,
edited by Philippa Algeo,
produced by Dragon's World,
phototypeset in Kennerley by
Apex Photosetting Limited
Colour Separation by Castlemead
Lithographic Reproduction Limited Hertford.

The captions and artwork in this
book have been supplied by the
entrants. Whilst every effort has
been made to ensure accuracy,
the Illustrators' Association does
not, under any circumstances,
accept responsibility for errors or
omissions.

A Dragon's World book
ISBN 0 905895 20 7

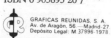

GRAFICAS REUNIDAS, S. A.
Av. de Aragón, 56. — Madrid-27
Depósito Legal: M 37996-1978

THE ASSOCIATION OF ILLUSTRATORS

In 1973 a group of illustrators and agents met to talk about their problems. They were concerned with the lack of uniform standards of professional conduct and misunderstandings between illustrators and their clients. As a result of this meeting the Association of Illustrators was formed, and, for the first time, illustrators had the machinery to improve their status in a number of ways.

Joyce Kirkland was appointed Director very shortly after the Association was formed and she, together with her assistant Nikki Hay, runs the business of the Association and its committees.

A voluntary committee of seven is appointed by the membership once a year and it meets every two weeks. Each member is responsible for a sub-committee: Exhibitions and the Annual, Ethics, Magazine, Education, Membership, Trade Unions and Forums. It is impossible to say that any one section has been responsible for the success of the Association, which has grown in under five years from a handful of artists to close on a thousand.

One of the aims of the AOI is to hold annually an exhibition of the best of British illustration. For this reason, all illustrators working in this country, whether they are members of the Association or not, are invited to submit their work. The Annual reproduces the work which the judges consider should be exhibited, and it is therefore the permanent record of the best of the year's work.

The Exhibition is now a major event, giving illustrators' work the necessary exposure and offering the artists an opportunity to sell original paintings. The Annual, with increasing sales each year, has become a necessary handbook to all who commission illustrations as well as giving the general public an insight into the work of the highly skilled illustrator whose talent is taken so much for granted.

The Ethics Committee is constantly busy and successfully solves the majority of cases brought to its attention. One example of this success is that the return of original artwork is now becoming the norm. In addition, the committee produced an AOI contract form and its increased use will rapidly decrease difficulties between artists and their clients.

Illustrators, the bi-monthly magazine, is available to all and non-members can obtain it on a subscription basis. It maintains a high standard and is both lively and informative.

The Education Sub-committee is mainly responsible for student membership and is available to offer help and advice while maintaining a regular dialogue with art colleges all over the country. It also organises tours of exhibitions when time and resources permit.

The work of the Trade Union Committee goes largely unsung. However, the Association can take credit for the fact that it has kept its members out of a union which, so far, has proved totally unsuitable for their needs.

Regular contact is maintained with Members of Parliament, lawyers, the TUC, the Publishers' Association and the Institute of Practitioners in Advertising. The patient and totally non-political negotiations of this branch of the AOI cannot be overstressed.

The Forums are held at the Association's offices on the last Thursday of every month and these meetings provide an excellent opportunity for illustrators to get to know one another and discuss common problems.

1978 has seen great strides forward. The Association moved its office from the Director's home to the Barley Mow Workspace at Chiswick, and the Director's Assistant, Nikki Hay, was appointed. With continued support from the membership, and the success of the 1978 Exhibition and Annual, the future is promising.

How to join the Association.
Write or telephone:
The Association of Illustrators,
10 Barley Mow Passage,
Chiswick,
London W4 4PH.
01-994 6477

ANNUAL

The Annual of the Association of Illustrators would not exist at all without a great deal of help from a large number of people. The judges were asked to give up precious weekend time, and the 35 eminent and busy individuals who agreed to serve spent a gruelling Sunday in April working from 10.30 am until 6.30 pm. They judged a record entry of 1,370 items, and they approached their task with dedication. To every one of them go the Association's sincere thanks for a task well done. Backing up the judges was a team of helpers who presented the work, operated the slide projectors, provided mountains of excellent food, dispensed fine wines and served endless cups of coffee... to you all, many thanks.

Alan Austin. The photograph above is a record of the judging day. From left to right;
Jacqui Dempsey, Arthur Robbins, David Christensen, Norman Messenger, Allan Manham, Tessa Farr, Eric Fairhead, Angela Landels, Brian Sanders, John Mundy, Faith Jaques, John Lawrence, Treld Bicknell, Shirley Hughes, John McConnell, Michele Beint, Donna Muir, John Gorham, Bush Hollyhead, Beverley Whitehead, John Barker, Chris Moore, Liz Moyes, Anne Huffman, Joyce Kirkland, Alan Austin, Philippa Algeo, Bob Norrington, Nikki Hay, Michael Hodgson, Posy Simmonds, Tracy Kirkland, Martin Richardson, Quentin Blake, Pearce Marchbank, Ken Kirkland, Tony Garrett, Visitor, Peter Brookes, Ross Thompson, Colin Cheeseman, Geoff Dunbar, Martin Lambie-Nairn, David McGrail, Gray Jolliffe, John Geary.

The Exhibition and Annual Sub-Committee
Alan Austin (Chairman), *Illustrator*
John Geary, *Illustrator*
Liz Moyes, *Illustrator*

ADVERTISING

Work commissioned for all spheres of advertising.

EDITORIAL

Work commissioned for magazines, periodicals and journals.

BOOK

Work commissioned for books and book covers.

PRINT AND DESIGN

Work commissioned for use in packaging, government services, architecture, medicine and other fields.

FILM AND TV

Work commissioned for use in film, TV, commercials, animation, storyboards, backgrounds, props and other associated media.

INDEX

AOI EXHIBITION JUDGES

ADVERTISING
David Christensen *Art Director,*
Boase Massimi Pollitt Univas
Jacqui Dempsey *Art Buyer,*
Foote Cone and Belding
Angela Landels *Illustrator*
Norman Messenger *Illustrator*
Arthur Robins *Illustrator*
Allan Manham *Illustrator*
Tessa Farr *Art Buyer,*
Benton and Bowles

EDITORIAL
Quentin Blake *Illustrator*
Peter Brookes *Illustrator*
Tony Garrett *Art Editor,*
New Society
Michael Hodgson *Assistant*
Art Editor, Harpers & Queen
Martin Richardson *Art Director,*
Woman's Own
Posy Simmonds *Cartoonist*
Pearce Marchbank *Art Director*
and Publisher

BOOK
Treld Bicknell *Art Editor,*
Kestrel Books
Enid Fairhead *Art Editor,*
Collins Childrens Books
Shirley Hughes *Illustrator*
Faith Jaques, *Illustrator*
John Lawrence *Illustrator*
John Munday *Art Director,*
Transworld Books
Brian Sanders *Illustrator*

PRINT/DESIGN
John Barker *Chairman,*
Artist Partners
Donna Muir *Illustrator*
John Gorham *Designer/Illustrator*
Bush Hollyhead *Illustrator*
John McConnell *Designer,*
Pentagram
Chris Moore *Illustrator*
Beverley Whitehead
Design Associate,
Michael Peters Partnership

"Why do agencies always play so safe when commissioning illustrations? Tried and tested solutions seem to be the criterion which is so different to the attitude shown by Continental art directors. British art directors always seem to play so safe.

Although he might be extremely experienced in using photography, the average art director is completely at sea when it comes to using illustration."
Allan Manham

1-51

"Several areas were, unfortunately poorly represented — notably newspaper illustration, illustration in the younger women's magazines, and fashion illustration. The younger women's magazines do not maintain a consistently high standard of illustration but they are always looking at and are prepared to use new work. They have been responsible for giving some of our best illustrators their first break."
Michael Hodgson

52-125

"I'm afraid there was the old problem of not enough good figure drawing, or of sensitive, straight interpretation of a text. Many illustrators who could have improved the standard in this area were, regrettably, absent."
Shirley Hughes

"I was less happy about the flood of science-fiction paperback covers we received. This ought to be an area where an artist's imagination could roam free — so why do so many of them look like machine-made clichés?"
Faith Jaques

126-236

"I was hoping to enjoy this section more than I did in the event. I know we were judging illustration only, but when you see jobs ruined by bad typography/design, it is very hard to enthuse about the work."
John Gorham

"The work submitted on 35mm transparencies divorced from a layout looked a great deal more impressive than when presented in printed form."
John Barker

237-282

"The work sent in under the Film and Television Section was, on the whole, most disappointing. It did not cover the range of work produced and more entries should be attracted."
Colin Cheeseman

283-292

The quotations above are extracts from the judges' comments.

TV AND FILM
Colin Cheeseman *Head of Graphic Design, BBC TV*
Geoff Dunbar *Animator, Grand Slam Animation*
Gray Jolliffe *Cartoonist*
Martin Lambie-Nairn *Graphic Designer, London Weekend TV*
Ross Thomson *Cartoonist*
Phil Mason *Art Director, BBDO*

ADVERTISING

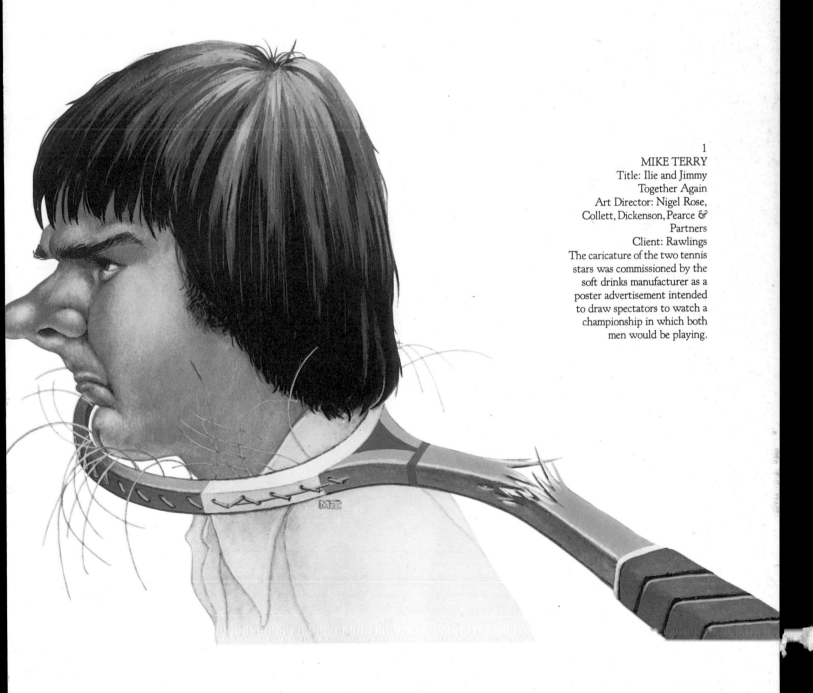

1
MIKE TERRY
Title: Ilie and Jimmy
Together Again
Art Director: Nigel Rose,
Collett, Dickenson, Pearce &
Partners
Client: Rawlings
The caricature of the two tennis
stars was commissioned by the
soft drinks manufacturer as a
poster advertisement intended
to draw spectators to watch a
championship in which both
men would be playing.

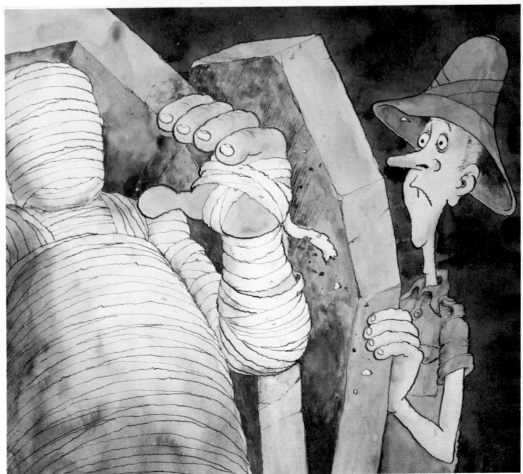

2, 3, 4
ARTHUR ROBINS
Rugby Players (above)
Gorilla (left)
Mummy (right)
Art Director: Paul Walter,
BBDO Ltd.
Client: Allied Breweries
(UK) Ltd.

5
GUY GLADWELL
Title: How Is China Managing
Without Mao? (above)

6
JOHN IRELAND
Title: Should The World Be
Running Out Of Energy? (right)
Art Director: John Hegarty,
TBWA
Client: Newsweek International
The oil painting (above)
measures 4′0″x4′0″and the
watercolour and crayon original
(right) measures 3′0″x3′0″.
Both were used to promote
Newsweek magazine in
consumer press. The brief in both
cases was to establish that the
magazine continually debates
world affairs.

Its more reliable with
Cable and Wireless

Its more reliable with
Cable and Wireless

Ken Thompson

Ken Thompson

7 8
KEN THOMPSON
Title: It's More Reliable with
Cable and Wireless
Art Director: Aziz Cami,
C S & S Design Partnership
Client: Cable and Wireless
These are two of a series of five
posters which appeared in the
Caribbean. They were executed
in watercolour and coloured
pencil.

9
DAN FERN
Title: Zoo
An unpublished painting
proposed for use as a poster for
Regents Park Zoo.

10
DAN FERN
Title: Art/Work
Client: The Association of
Illustrators
A poster advertising an
exhibition of illustration at the
the National Theatre, London.

11
STUART BODEK
Title: Printer's Nightmare (right)
Art Director: Agneta Halen
Client: Appelgeldt Werne Co.
The illustration depicts a
printing press rejecting old
paper, and crashing out of the
machine shop. It will not return
until a new brand of paper
is used.

LONDON ZOO REGENTS PARK OPEN DAILY

ART/WORK

AN EXHIBITION OF PRELIMINARY DRAWINGS
AND ARTWORK BY PROFESSIONAL AND
STUDENT ILLUSTRATORS, ORGANISED BY THE
ASSOCIATION OF ILLUSTRATORS, AT THE
NATIONAL THEATRE, SOUTH BANK, MONDAY
16 JANUARY TO SATURDAY 25 FEBRUARY 1978

Rubus Dasyphyllus

12
CHRIS MOORE
Title: Honey Bee
Art Director: Nick Daniels,
McBride Partnership

Apis Mellifera

13
GRAHAME THOMPSON
Title: Traffic Jam
Art Director: Peter Hughes
J Walter Thompson Co. Ltd.
Client: Electricity Council
The illustration formed part of a
national press campaign for the
Electricity Council together
with the slogan 'Ever thought of
traffic without the lights?'

14
JOHN THOMPSON
Title: Letraline Poster
Art Director: Brian M Dedman,
Butler Cornfield Dedman Ltd.
Client: Letraset International
A design for a poster which was
to show the use of Letraline in
the cartographic and planning
fields. Since the poster was to
be used internationally, the
product had to be promoted
with a minimum of words.

15
ALAN CRACKNELL
Title: See It Our Way
Art Director: Andy Arghyrou,
Fletcher Shelton Delaney
Reynolds Ltd.
Client: Iran Air
One of a series of posters for
specially designed window
display units in travel agents in
the United Kingdom and Europe.
The painting was produced in
five colours with additional

gold printing to simulate the
traditional style of Persian
miniatures.

16
TERRY WRIGHT
Title: Hedge
Art Director: Clinton Firth,
TBWA
Client: Wolverhampton &
Dudley Breweries

One of a series of paintings
which show a Banks' and
Hanson's drinker who has cele-
brated reaching the Milestone
by creating the milestone logo
out of his natural surroundings —
in this case the hedge.

17
PAULINE ELLISON
Title: Mermaid (above)
Art Director: Tony Muranka/
Ken Mullen, J Walter Thompson
Co. Ltd.
Client: Hedges and Butler Ltd.

18
PAULINE ELLISON
Title: Black Christmas
Art Director: Charlotte
Sherwood, TBWA
Client: John Walker and
Sons Ltd.
The artist was commissioned to
paint a classic Christmas land-
scape for the distiller's Christmas
advertising campaign.

19
WAYNE ANDERSON
Title: Castles (above right)
Art Director: Tony Muranka/
Ken Mullen, J Walter Thompson
Co. Ltd.
Client: Hedges and Butler Ltd.

20
PETER LE VASSEUR
Title: Cats and Dogs (right)
Art Director: Tony Muranka/
Ken Mullen, J Walter Thompson
Co. Ltd.
Client: Hedges and Butler Ltd.

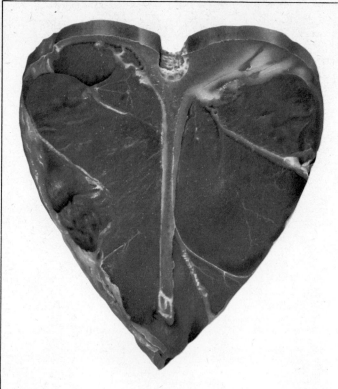

21
PAUL HIGGINS
Title: Heart of Steak
Client: Pran & Torgesen
The illustration was com-
missioned by a Norwegian
farmers' meat marketing
organisation. The artist was
asked to depict sirloin steak
realistically for use in a poster
designed to convince the general
public of their love for steak.

22, 23
JENNY POWELL
Title: Girl's Head (above)
Title: Girl in Evening Dress
(below left)
Both of these unpublished, self-

promotional drawings were
executed in conte pencil and
watercolour on an emulsion
base. The girl in evening dress
drawing is 20" high, while the
head is 8½" x 7½".

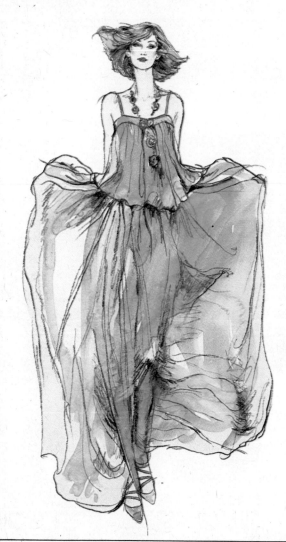

24
DUTHY DUBRULE
Untitled
Art Director: Alan Williams
Client: Harvey Nichols
The client was interested in the
atmosphere of the drawings and
trusted the artist to note the
essential fashion details. The
original drawing was 18" high,
and the medium was conte
pencil.

COLIN HADLEY   Art Director: Alan Morrow,

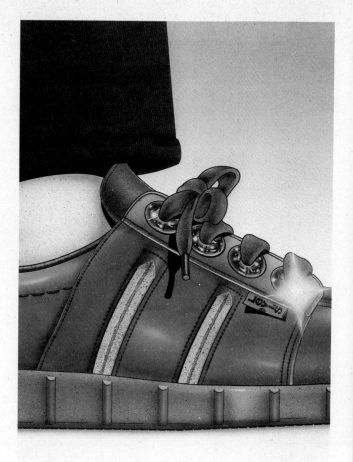

26
PHIL DOBSON
Title: Look Right Into Our Eyes
Art Director: Eric Barker,
McCann Erickson
Advertising Ltd.
Client: Levi's
One of three posters used for
the 'Levi's for feet' advertising
campaign on London's under-
ground stations. Original size:
390mm x 540mm.

27
DAVID HOLMES
Title: Full Circle
Art Director: Brenda Jobbling,
Lonsdale Crowther
Osborne Ltd.
The painting was commissioned
for an advertising poster for the
thriller film of the same name,
starring Mia Farrow.

28
ALAN AUSTIN
Title: Cabbages
Art Director: Bennie Cross,
John Brimacombe & Co.

Client: Erin Foods
This illustration was one of a
series drawn for packaging of a
range of freeze-dried vegetables.
The brief called for a drawing

that would suggest freshness and
to fit into a tight, type-dominated
space.

29
MICK BROWNFIELD
Title: Seven Home Runs A Day
(above)
Art Director: Mike Preston,
J Walter Thompson Co. Ltd.
Client: Pan American World
Airways Inc.

30
NICHOLAS JOHN
THOMPSON
Title: Amin/Snake
A self-promotional mailing shot
printed from two, same size,
originals on tracing paper. After
the illustrations had been completed in ink, razor blades were
used to etch texture and patterns
into them.

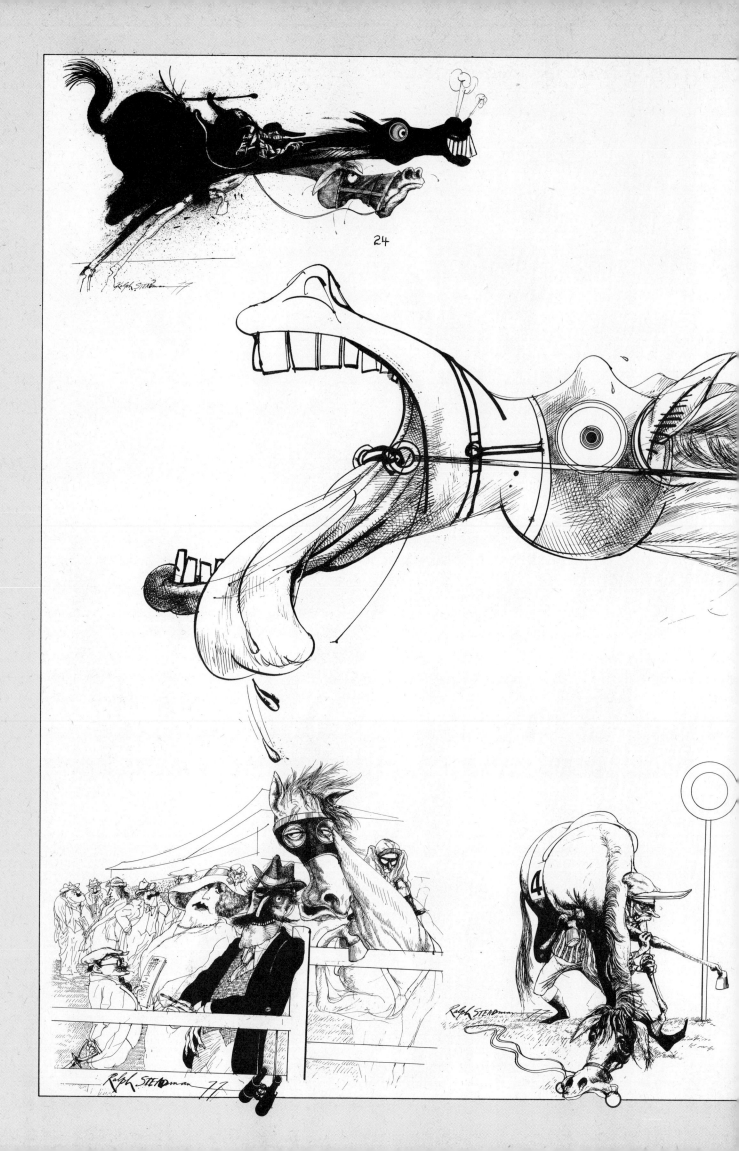

24

RALPH STEADMAN
Art Director: Mike Garwood,
Benton and Bowles
Client: The Joe Coral Group
Four drawings for a national
press advertising campaign.

32
STEVE PICKARD
Title: Ice-Cream With Delight
Art Director: Chris McEwan
This self-promotional piece was
an exercise in using flat colours
with black outlines.

33
STEVE PICKARD
Title: Free-Falling Fantasy
Art Director: Soo Williams
An unpublished work in which
the artist wanted to use as many
bright colours as possible.

34
MANCHUELLE DESHAYES
Title: Dry Cane—Swimming
Pool (top left)
Dry Cane—Interior (above)
Art Director: David Christensen,
Boase Massimi Pollitt
Client: Saccone and Speed

35
HARRY HANTS
Art Director: Mark Williams,
French Gold Abbott
Client: Saxa Salt

36
PAMELA CRESWELL
Title: Having A Wonderful Wish
Time You Were Here
One of a series of observations
executed in similar style for the
artist's BA degree folio

37
PETER GOODFELLOW
Title: Gulliver
Art Director: Charles Cooper,
Allen Brady and Marsh
Client: Whitbread & Co. Ltd.

38
ROY KNIPE
Title: Rucksack
Art Director: Kees de Wijn
Client: Durex
A full-colour painting for a
poster appealing to young people
going on holiday. The drawing
was reproduced at twice the
size of the original

39
JOHN HOLDER
Title: 13th Cambridge Folk
Festival Poster
Art Director: Gaye Lockwood
Client: Cambridge City Council

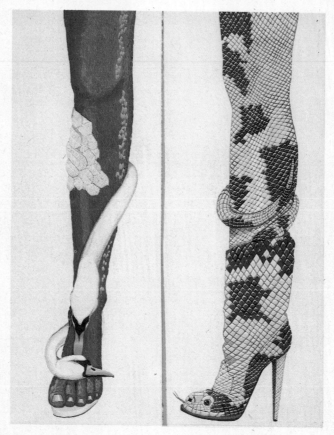

40
BRIAN GRIMWOOD
Title: The Penguin (top left)
Bird on a Branch (top right)
The Rabbit (left)
The Ginger Cat (right)
Art Director: Brian Grimwood
Client: Yorke Rosenberg and
Mardall
Four of twelve pictures
commissioned for the restaurant
at London Gatwick Airport.

41
TRUDIE-JANE BELLINGER
Title: Legs

42
JOHN BUTLER
Title: Still Life in the Old
Bird Yet
Art Director: Per Manning,
Pran & Torgesen
A poster illustration showing
a new range of Norwegian
liver patés.

43
MIKE TERRY
Title: Premium Bonds (above)
Art Director: Mike Crossley,
Saatchi & Saatchi Compton
This painting was commissioned
for use in promoting Premium
Bonds.

44
MICK BROWNFIELD
Title: Sweet Pea (left)
Art Director: Jenni Stone
Client: Jenni Stone Agency
A promotional illustration for
the agency's mail-out.

45
RAY WINDER
Title: Faultless Furnishings
(above)
Art Director: Bill Greaves
Client: Aston Martin
A watercolour illustration of
the interior of the Aston Martin
V8 for use in a brochure.

46
MICHAEL FRITH
Title: Jeff Thompson (left)
A watercolour and crayon illus-
tration of a sports personality.
Original size: 7" x 13".

47
JOOCE GARRETT
Title: Interior of Amsterdam
canal house (left)
Interior of Amsterdam bar
(right)
Art Director: Tejo Hollander,
Franzen Hey and Veltman
Client: Heineken Bier

The paintings were done for
Dutch press advertisements.
Medium: Acrylics.

48
KEN THOMPSON
Title: Elephants (above)
Art Director: Bernard Miles
(right), Bruce Gill (left), Fletcher,
Shelton, Delaney, Reynolds Ltd.
Client: Sketchley Cleaners
The artwork was used as on-
window four-sheet posters.
Sketchley wanted to give their
shops some colour and humour,
as well as reminding the public
that they offer quality and value.

49
JULIAN GRADDON
Title: Jack and Jill (above right)

50, 51
CECIL VIEWEG
Untitled (left and right)
Art Director: Rod Taylor
Client: Davidson, Pearce, Berry
and Spottiswood
A double page spread illustration
of a father with two children,
and the mother working in the
kitchen.

52
PETER BROOKES
Title: Beauty and the Beast
Art Editor: Clive Crook
Client: The Sunday Times
Magazine
The artist was asked to illustrate
an article on the destruction of
various species of animals to
provide materials for the fashion
and cosmetics industries.
Medium: Gouache. Original
size: 13½″ x 6¼″.

EDITORIAL

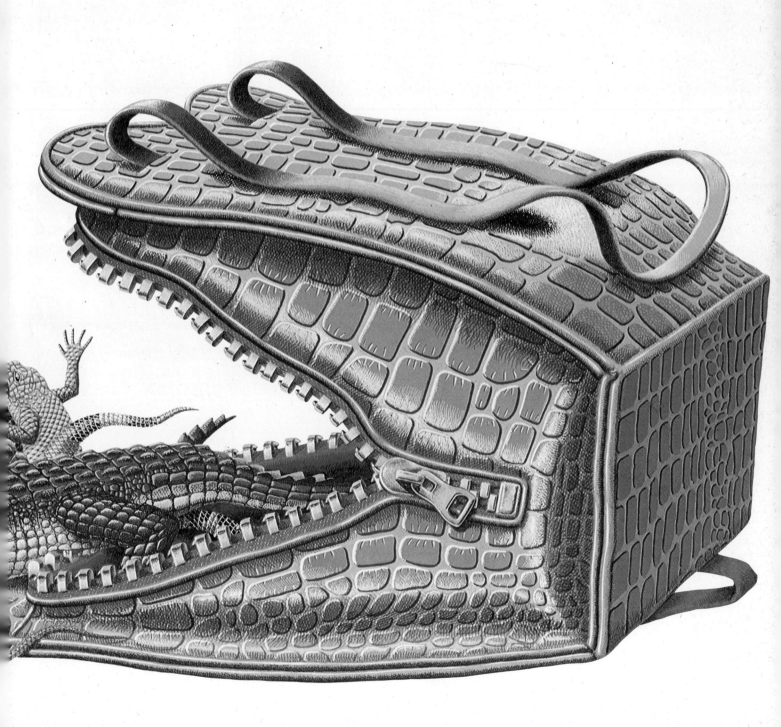

53
DAVE FARWELL SMITH
Title: This is London
Art Director: Ken Taylor
A drawing of central London
showing cinemas, theatres, and
streets for *A Survival Guide For
Visitors*. Medium: inks. Original
size approximately 30″ wide.

54
NICHOLAS HARDCASTLE
Title: View from a Train

55
TERENCE DALLEY
Title: The Little Villa
One of a series of studies of the
architecture of English seaside,
holiday and retirement homes.
Medium: Gouache. Original
size: 15½cm x 20½cm.

56
MARTIN NEWTON
Title: Windmill
Media: Oil, pastel and ink.

57
NICHOLAS HARDCASTLE
Title: Town and Country
The illustration shows the reflection of countryside in the window of a Rolls Royce showroom.

58
ALAN BAINES
Title: Grand National
The gouache painting was executed as a self-promotional piece.

60
PETER HOLT
Title:"Out of sight..." (above)

59
PETER TILL
Title: Ten-Pin Bowling (top)
Art Director: Pearce Marchbank
Client: Time Out Magazine
A drawing for the cover of the
magazine illustrating an article
on ten-pin bowling in London.

Peter Till.

61
PETER TILL
Title: Bad Briefing
Art Director: Dave Curless
Client: Campaign Magazine
An illustration for an article on
the necessity of a good briefing
from an advertising agency's
client..

62, 63
CHRISTINE ROCHE
Title: The Intermittent
Husband Syndrome
Ghost Marriages
Art Director: Tony Garrett
Client: New Society

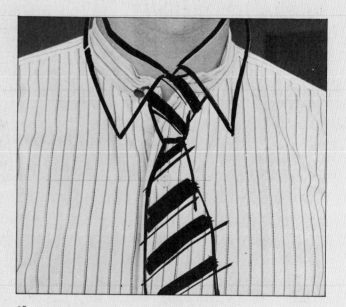

64
JOHN GEARY
Title: The Experience of
Abortion
Art Director: Tony Garrett

Client: New Society
The brief for the cover illustration was tight and does not
represent the artist's view

65
EDWARD BELL
Title: Conservative Social
Policy
Art Director: Tony Garrett

Client: New Society
The artist drew the collar and
tie over a photograph of a collar-
less shirt.

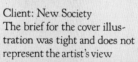

66
ANTHONY KERINS
Title: Crossfire!
Art Director: Terry Dowling
Client: Film Form
The illustration for a magazine
article and a film was done in
fountain pen and wash. The
original was 15 cm x 21 cm.

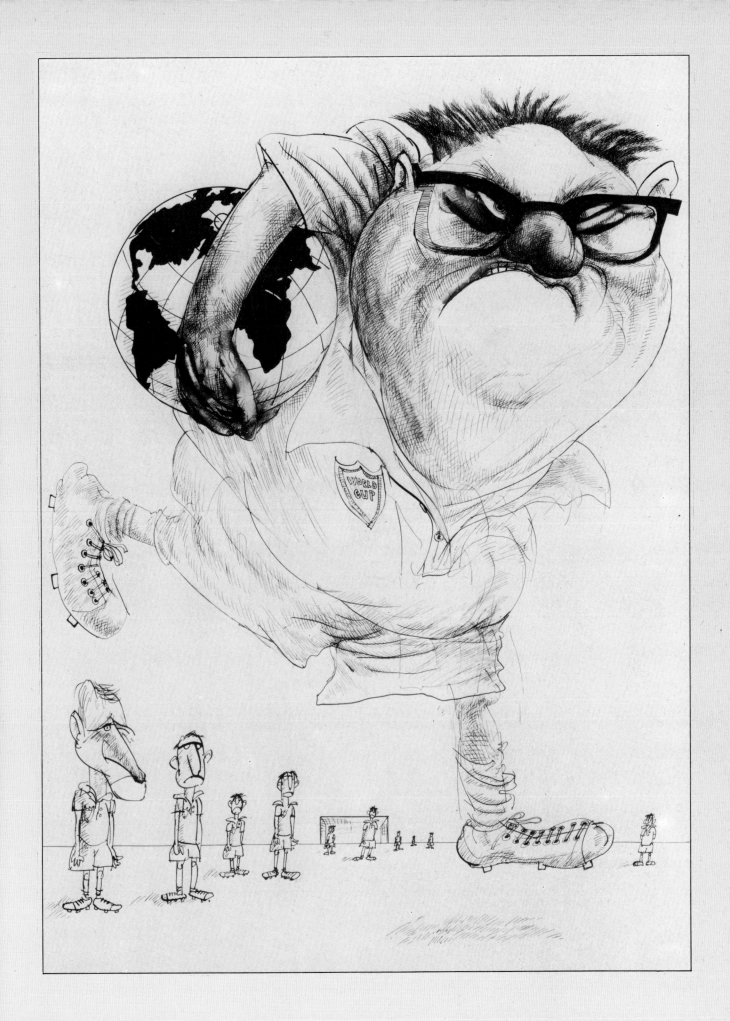

67
RALPH STEADMAN
Title: Dr Kissinger
Art Editor: David Driver
Client: The Radio Times

68
PETER BROOKES
Title: The Good Life Guide
(top)
Art Director: Michael Rand
Client: The Sunday Times
Magazine
The illustration accompanied a
quiz on health and ageing.
Medium: Pen and Ink.
Original size: 10½″ x 6¾.″

69
LYNDA GRAY
Title: Stumped For
A Good Read
Art Editor: Clive Crook
Client: The Sunday Times
Magazine
The painting accompanied an
article about books on cricket.
Media: Gouache and water-
colour.

70
PETER BROOKES
Title: Chinese Week
Art Director: David Driver
Client: Radio Times

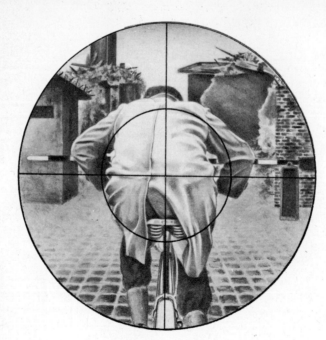

71
PETER KNOCK
Title: Designs On You (top)
Art Director: Derek Ungless
Client: BBC Publications
An illustration for a series of
programmes on the role of the
designer in the community.

72
PETER KNOCK
Title: The Spy Who Came In
From The Cold
Art Editor: Brian Thomas
Client: BBC Publications
An illustration to the opening
chapter of John Le Carre's book
of the same title which was
serialised for radio.

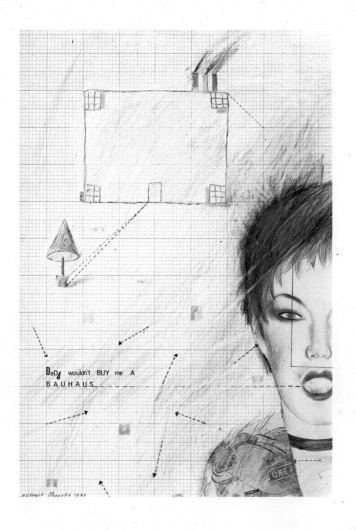

73
LAWRENCE MYNOTT
Title: DADA Wouldn't Buy
Me A Bauhaus (top left)
Art Director: John Hind/
Jenny Beeston
Client: ARK '54
A drawing illustrating an article
written by Professor Guyatt.

74
LAWRENCE MYNOTT
Title: Even Heads of Departments Have to Relax Sometime.
Professor Richard Guyatt
(top right)
One of a proposed series of
drawings of members of staff at
the artist's art college.

75
BRIAN SANDERS
Title: The Water Filter
Art Director: Martin Richardson
Client: Woman's Own Magazine
An illustration for a short story
about a young girl who puts a
frog into a water filter in order
to frighten an unpopular cousin.

76
PAULINE ELLISON
Art Director: David Driver
Client: Radio Times

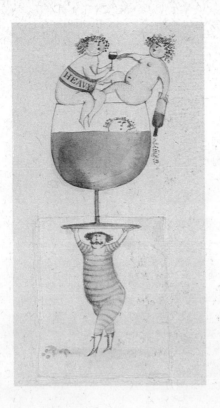

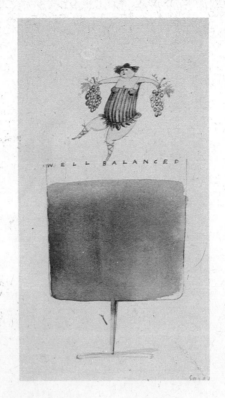

77
SARAH MIDDA
Title: Wine Bibber's Vocabulary
Art Editor: Clive Crook
Client: Sunday Times Magazine

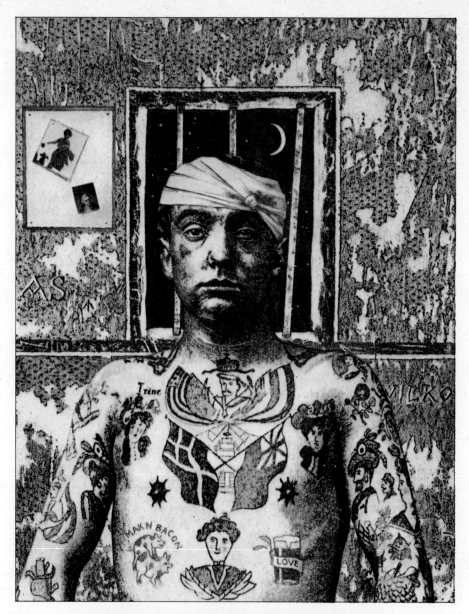

78
TONY McSWEENEY
Title: Remember Hull 1976?
Art Director: John Carrod
Client: National Council for
Civil Liberties
A black-and-white illustration
to an article in the Council's
Rights magazine on the Hull
prison riots in 1976. Media:
Pencil, collage. 153mm x 120mm.

79
LEO DUFF
Title: Warehouse in Southwark
One of a set of drawings of
buildings in Southwark. Media:
Pencil, gum and varnish.
Original size: 80cm x 38cm.

80
BRIAN SANDERS
Title: Bewitched
Art Director: Martin Richardson
Client: Woman's Own Magazine
A single page illustration for a
short story about three young
girls on Halloween Eve hoping
for an insight of the men they
will eventually marry.

81,82
CHLOE CHEESE
Title: Al Fresco A La Francaise
(above)
Beginners' Guide to the Grape
(right)
Art Editor: Clive Crook
Client: Sunday Times Magazine

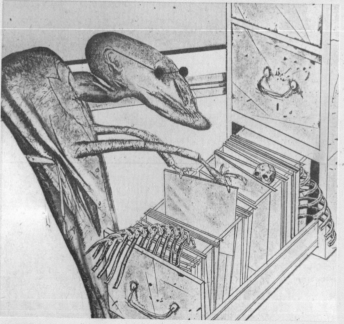

83, 84, 85
IAN POLLOCK
Title: Two Whores (top)
An unpublished drawing
prompted by the artist's horror
at the sight of the prostitutes on
Rue St Denis, Paris. The drawing
has since been linked into a
series of Old Testament
illustrations.
Title: Skeletons In The
Cupboard (left)
Art Director: John Carrod
Client: National Council for
Civil Liberties

A pencil drawing for an article
in *Rights,* the newspaper of the
N.C.C.L. This 7½″ x 6½″ illustration is a collage of photostats
of pencil drawings which are
then photocopied again and the
resulting copy is worked into
with a soft pencil and rubber.
Title: The Mime of Mick, Nick,
and the Maggies (right)
Art Director: Brian Thomas
Client: Radio Times
A pencil drawing illustration of
a Radio 3 play.

86
IAN POLLOCK
Title: Alcoholics
Art Director: Mike von Joel

Client: New Styles
The original illustration was a very faint drawing which the artist photocopied to bring up

the grain. The copy was then worked with a soft pencil, glue and a toothbrush.

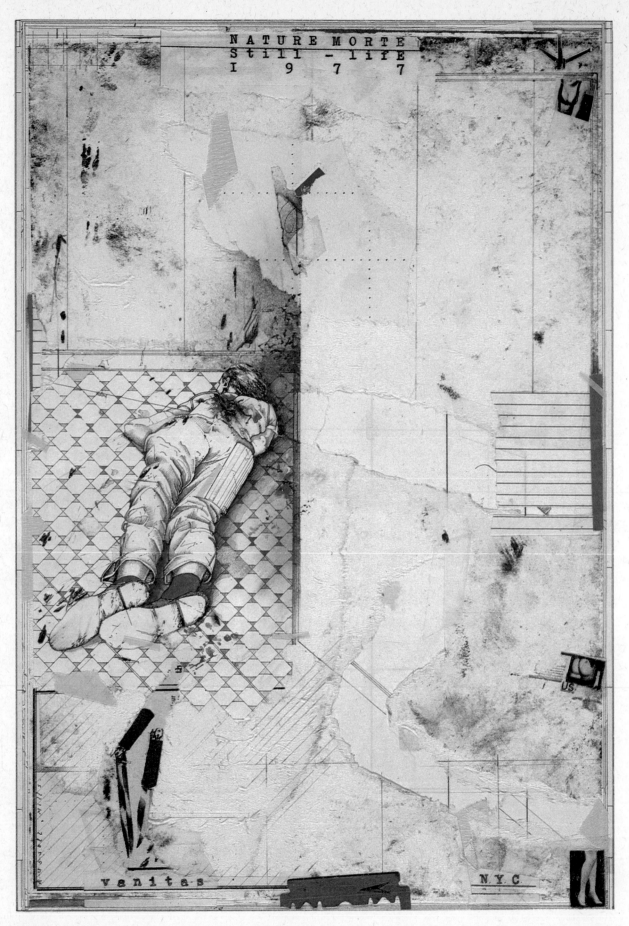

87
RUSSELL MILLS
Title: Still Life/Nature Morte
N.Y.C. (above)
Art Director: Mike van Joel
Client: New Styles
A mixed media collage, 11¼" x
7¾", with colour but published
in black and white.

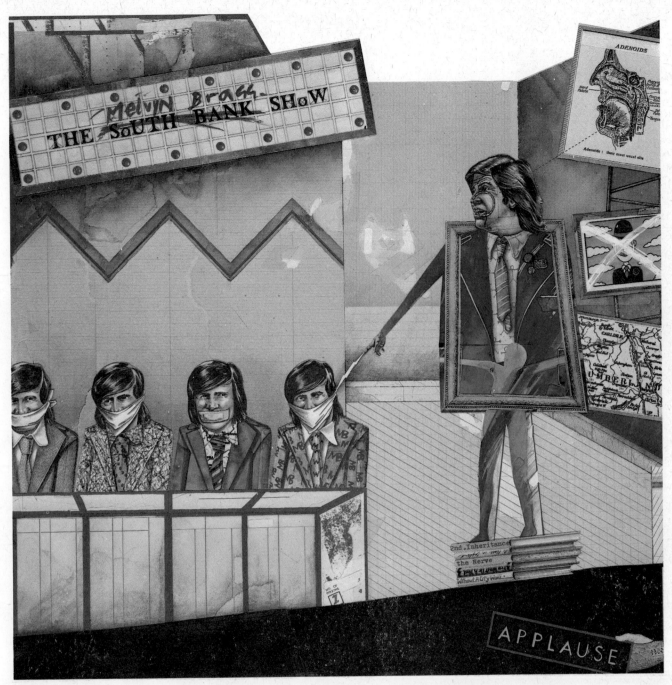

88
RUSSELL MILLS
Title: Melvyn Is So Modest
(above)
Art Editor: Clive Crook
Client: Sunday Times Magazine
The illustration accompanies a
lampoon of Melvyn Bragg. The
artist doubled the satire by
basing the work on a painting
by David Hockney called *A
Grand Procession of Dignitaries
in the Semi-Egyptian Style,*
which in its turn is a parody of
style. Mixed media collage.

89
RUSSELL MILLS
Title: Age of Uncertainty
Art Editor: Brian Thomas
Client: Radio Times
This was the first of a set of 13
illustrations done to accompany
a weekly series in which
Professor Galbraith gave a
personal view of all aspects of
economics since Adam Smith.
The artwork was executed for
mono reproduction with spot-
colour overlay.

ILLUSTRATORS

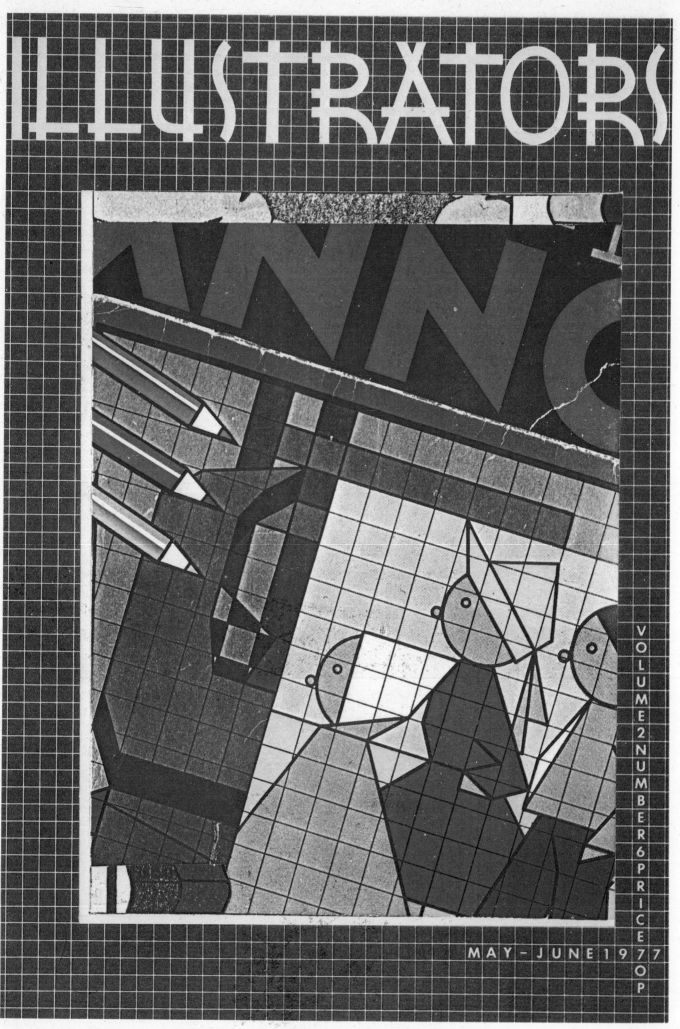

VOLUME2NUMBER6PRICE0P

MAY-JUNE1977

90 DAN FERN Title: Illustrators Art Director: Dan Fern Client: Association of Illustrators Two cover designs for the Association's magazine.

ILLUSTRATORS

VOLUME 2 NUMBER 6 PRICE 70P

MAY – JUNE 1977

91
TONY MEEUWISSEN
Title: Gulliver (right)
Art Editor: Brian Thomas
Client: Radio Times
A drawing for BBC Radio 4
Story Time series on *Gulliver's Travels*.

92,93
BILL SANDERSON
Title: Jacques Cousteau—
Technological Merman (above)
Title: The Question Must Be
Asked (right)
Art Editor: Brian Thomas
Client: Radio Times

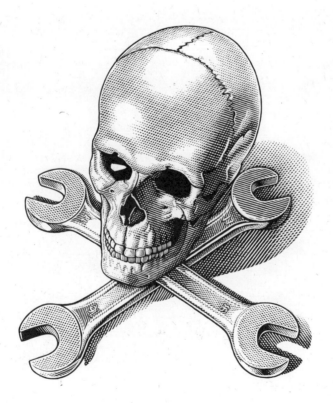

94
TERENCE DALLEY
Title: London Demolition
This was one of a series of
paintings recording the changing
face of London. The building was
in Park Lane.

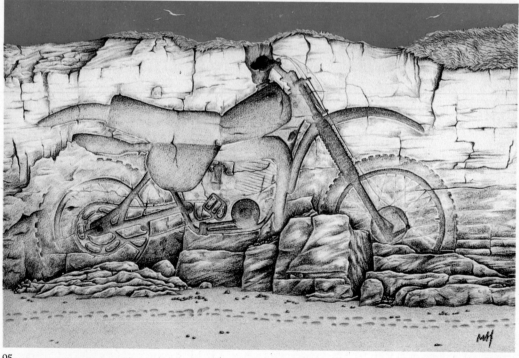

95
MALCOLM HENWOOD
Title: Fossilized Motorcycle
The illustration was executed
for a college project in which the
brief was to produce a full-colour
illustration for a magazine article.

96, 97
BRIAN GRIMWOOD
Title: Where Your Treasure Is ...
(top)
Art Director: Joy Hannington
Client: Homes and Gardens
Magazine

Title: Parties
Art Director: Keith Jones
Client: Over 21 Magazine
A front cover illustration for a
pull-out booklet.

98
DAVE EASTBURY
Title: The Housewife (top)
The illustration was executed to
a college project brief. It shows
the idea that housework is hard,
time consuming and boring.
Black and white gouache.
Original size: 12"x15½."

99
POSY SIMMONDS
Art Director: Ken Ellis
Client: Readers' Digest
A decorative heading for a
regular magazine feature.

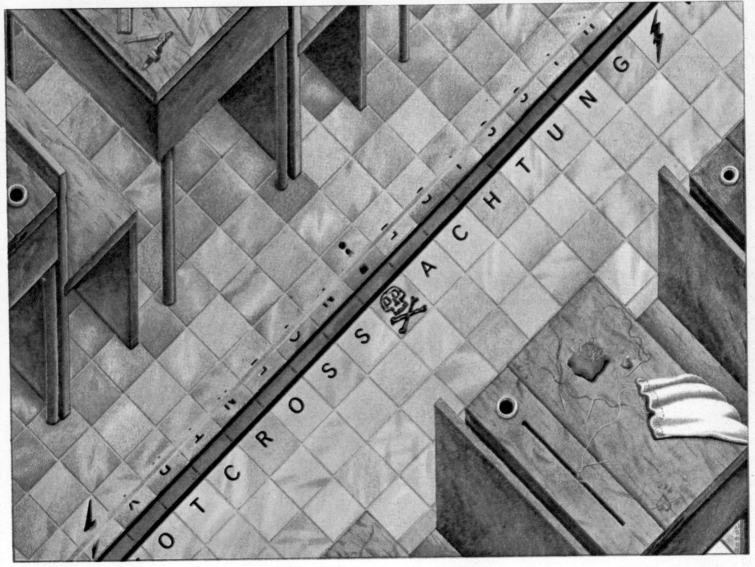

100, 101
ROBERT MASON
Title: A Man's Place Is In The
Home (above)
Art Editor: Clive Crook
Client: Sunday Times Magazine

Title: Why Our Education
System Is Unfair To Women
Art Editor: Clive Crook
Client: Sunday Times Magazine

102
NORMAN WEAVER
Title: Aquarium Fishes
Art Editor: Clive Crook
Client: Sunday Times Magazine
A double page spread of warm
and cool water fishes for a home
aquarium.

103
CLARE MARTIN
Title: Colourful Cooking
A full-colour illustration
executed as a specimen for the
artist's portfolio. Original size:
185 mm x 200 mm.

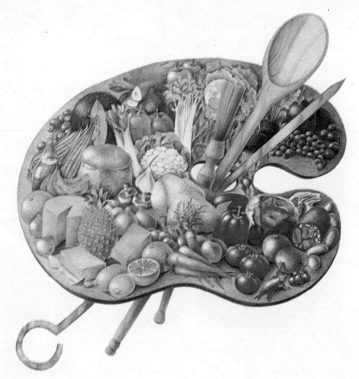

104
DAVID PENNEY
Title: Barns
Art Editor: Clive Crook
Client: Sunday Times Magazine
A composite, exploded view
showing typical features of
barns. Media: Watercolour.

105
DONNA MUIR
Title: Sacred Cows: American
Literature
Art Editor: Clive Crook
Client: Sunday Times Magazine

106
DAVID R. DAVIES
Title: The Banana Addict
A pen and ink watercolour
illustration of the theme 'Food'
for an exhibition organised by
the Royal College of Art.
Original size: 210mm x 180mm.

"my wife and..."

in the hours that were spent, as the ROLLS came and went. P.M.

107
DONNA MUIR
Paul McCartney
Art Editor: Clive Crook
Client: Sunday Times Magazine

108, 109
ROBIN JACQUES
Title: Bible Lands: Noah's Ark
(top left)
Bible Lands: And the Frogs
Came Up (right)
Art Editor: Brian Thomas
Client: Radio Times
The illustrations were done for a
television series which compared
Biblical narrative with con-
temporary archaeological
evidence. The artist's brief was
to provide a graphic reminder
of the Bible stories.

110
JULIAN GRADDON
Title: Malcolm Muggeridge
(top right)
The painting, done in acrylic and
gouache, was a private
commission.
Original size: 190 m x 95 cm.

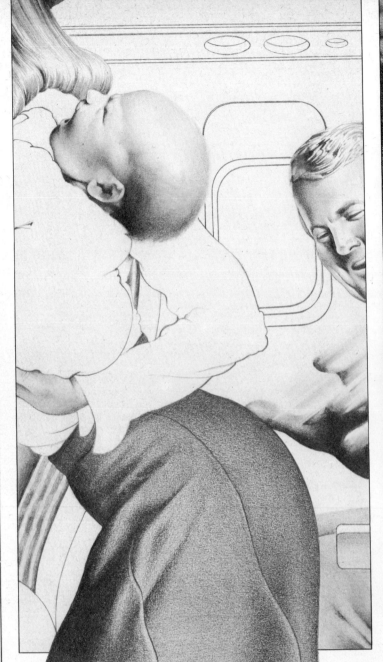

111
BILL PROSSER
Art Director: Rob Prosser
Client: IPC/Honey Magazine
A pencil drawing illustrating a
feature article entitled 'Those

Glamorous Jobs Are Not All
They're Cracked Up To Be'.

112
MURIEL MACKENZIE
Title: John's Wife
Art Director: Tony Garrett
Client: New Society

113
GEORGE HARDIE
Title: The Illustrators'
Christmas Ball
Art Director: Michael Hodgson
Client: The Association of
Illustrators
A cover painting for the magazine
of the Association.

114
ADRIAN GEORGE
Title: Tony Van Den Bergh
Art Editor: Brian Thomas
Client: Radio Times
The subject had for many years
been a producer and reporter
for the BBC specialising in
medical programmes. After he
had undergone a serious opera-
tion himself the artist portrayed
him in a wheelchair.

115
GEORGE HARDIE
Title: Vision of the Future
Art Director: David Driver
Client: Radio Times
A cover illustration for the
magazine which contained an
article on television of the future.

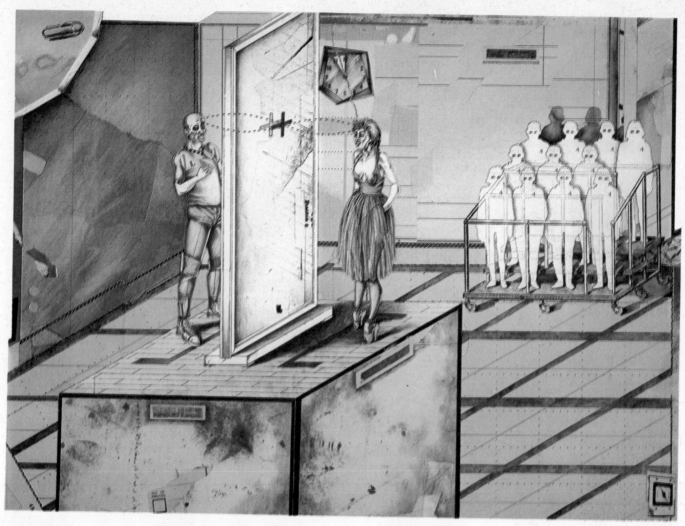

116
RUSSELL MILLS
Title: The Aquarian Age
Art Director: Michael Hodgson
Client: Harpers and Queen
Magazine
A mixed-media collage,

117
CHRISTOPHER SHARROCK
Title: Even Heads of Departments
Have to Relax Sometime
One of a proposed series of ink
drawings of members of staff in
Liverpool Polytechnic's Graphic
Design Department.

118
IAN POLLOCK
Title: Two Drinkers
Art Director: Philip Dunn
Client: Pierrot Publishing Ltd.
One of 60 pen, ink and rapido-
graph drawings for a book by the
artist entitled Couples.

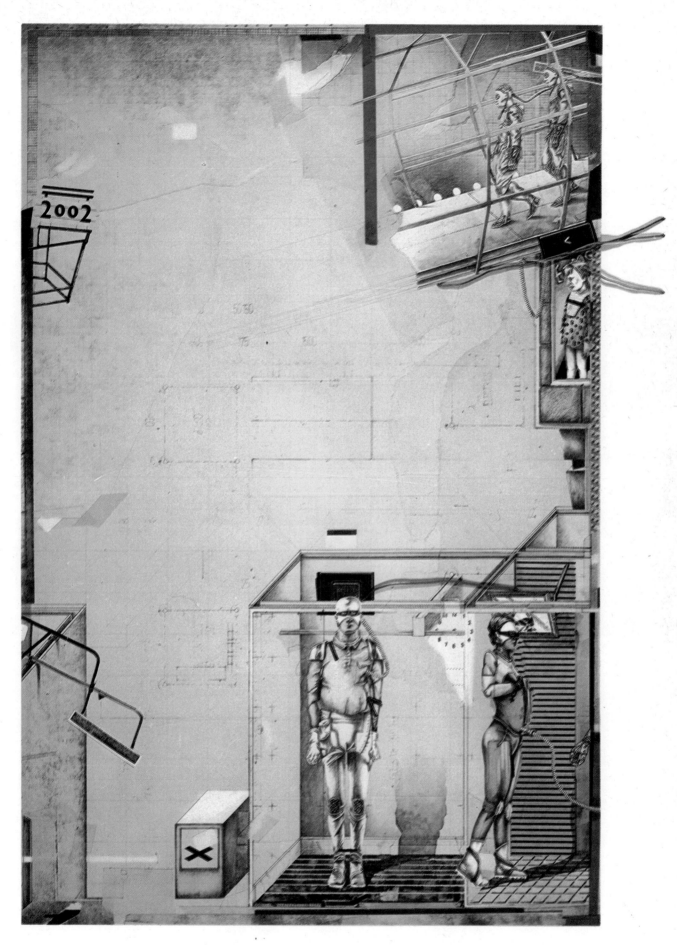

119
RUSSELL MILLS
Title: Society 2002
The brief was to provide an
image of society in 2002. The
artist decided to confine the
emphasis to selected references
to a modern 'Metropolis' rather
than a 'Utopia'.

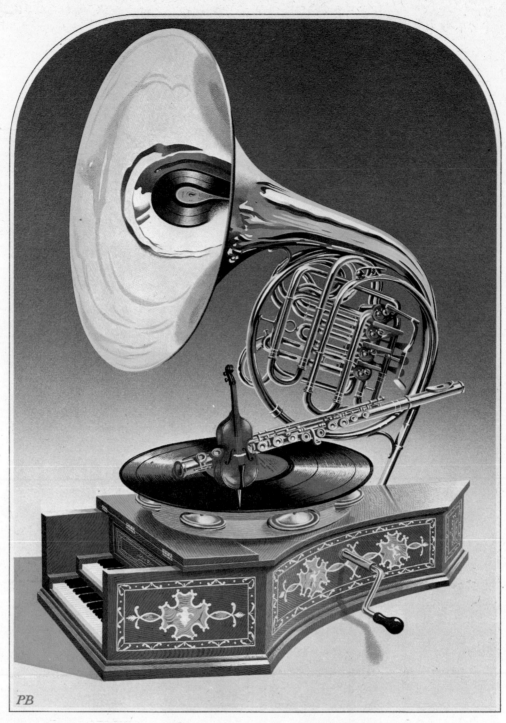

120
PETER BROOKES
Title: Classic Collection
(top)
Art Editor: Clive Crook
Client: Sunday Times Magazine
The 'Classic Collection' was
designed to illustrate an article
which was a guide for beginners
when building a classical record
collection.

121
PETER BROOKES
Title: Slow Sellers of '77
Art Director: Edwin Taylor
Client: The Sunday Times
The brief was to provide a
drawing which illustrated an
article on the topic of books
doomed not to become best
sellers.

122
PETER BROOKES
Sacred Cows: Called to the Bar
Art Editor: Clive Crook
Client: Sunday Times Magazine

123,124,125
MICK BROWNFIELD
Title: Not in front of the
the Children
(above)
Art Editor: Clive Crook
Client: Sunday Times Magazine

Title: Lucky Strikes
(right)
Art Director: Peter Baistow
Client: Design Council
A cover illustration for design
magazine.

Title: C3PO and
Robert Mitchum
(far right)
Art Director: Pierce Marchbank
Client: Time Out Magazine
Cover illustration for Christmas
Issue.

BOOK

126
LOUISE VOCE
Title: Dogs
Preliminary drawings in watercolour and ink on the character
of the dog in the story *The Cat
that Walked by Himself.*

127
IAN POLLOCK
Title: Twins in Bed
Art Director: Philip Dunn
Client: Pierrot Publishing Ltd.
A watercolour illustration for a
science fiction novel, *Brothers of
the Head* by Brian W. Aldiss.

128
PETER TILL
Title: Socialist Propaganda In
The Twentieth Century British
Novel
Art Director: Cherriwyn Magill
Client: Macmillan & Co. Ltd.
The artist was asked to provide
an imaginative solution which
interpreted the title of the book.
Medium: Pen. Original size:
220 mm x 340 mm.

129
SIMON STERN
Title: Mrs Vinegar
Illustrations for a folktale with
the hand lettering done by the
artist.

130
CHRIS McEWAN
Title: Snakes and Ladders
A double page spread illustration
for a poster-sized book on
children's games. The numbered
board, snakes, ladders and other
characters are drawn on a jungle
background.

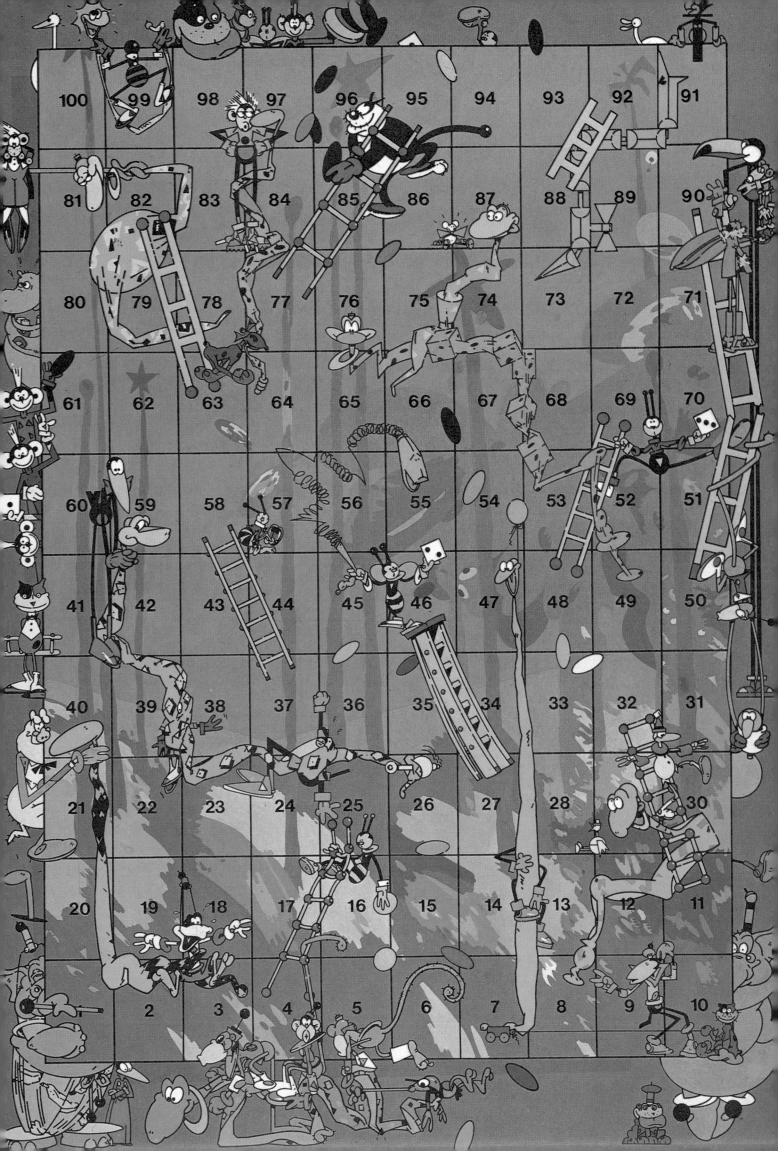

131, 132
CHRIS McEWAN
Title: Daffy Daggles
A watercolour illustration for
the cover of a children's fantasy
story book. Original size: 10″x 8.″
Untitled (left)
One page from a poster-sized
book on children's games.
Medium: Poster paints.
Original size: 21″x 26.″

Boldly Illustrated by Arthur Robins.

133,134
ARTHUR ROBINS
Title: At The Height of The
Moon (top)
Asimov's Lecherous Limericks
(left)
Art Director: John Munday
Client: Transworld
Publishers Ltd.

135
SALLY HOLMES
Title: Wraggle Taggle War
Art Director: Olga Noris
Client: Abelard-Schuman Ltd.
A book jacket illustration for a
children's story. The original
artwork is 21″ x 11½″ and was
executed in watercolour,
coloured inks and crayon.

136
DOROTHY LOAN
An unpublished drawing of a
window from the inside looking
out with a variety of objects on
a table in front. Media: Watercolour and pencil.

137, 138 ,139
KATY SLEIGHT
Title: Dick's Store (top left)
Chicken Run (top right)
Steyning High Street
All three illustrations are water-
colours and are unpublished.

140
PETER BROOKES
Title: The Hermit of Peking
Art Director: David Pelham
Client: Penguin Books
This book jacket illustration,
done in the style of a Chinese
lacquered screen, was to show
the hermit in an anthropo-
morphic landscape. Medium:
Gouache. Original size: 5½″ x 9.″

141
TONY RANDELL
Title: Sunday Times Best
British Meat Dishes
Designer: John Tennant
Client: Sunday Times Magazine/
Cassells

142
CHRIS MOORE
Title: A Choice Of Gods
Art Director: Peter Bennett
Client: Magnum Paperbacks

143
PETER ANDREW JONES
Title: Orn
Art Director: John Munday
Client: Transworld
Publishers Ltd.
A wrap-around paperback book
cover illustration in oils on hard-
board. Original size: 16" x 24".

144, 145
PETER ANDREW JONES
Title: Inferno
Art Director: Dom Rodi
Client: Alan Wingate Ltd.
A hardback, wrap-around dust
jacket illustration in oil and
acrylic on hardboard repre-
senting the three giants that
guard the devil in Dante's
Inferno.

Title: The Storm Lord
Art Director: Patrick Mortemore
Client: Futura Publications Ltd.
The illustration was based on an
idea worked out by the artist
and the art director. The per-
spective was distorted to fit the
book cover. Media: Acrylic and
oil. Original size: 28″ x 20″.

146
PETER MORTER
Untitled
Art Director: Roger Bristow
Client: Dorling Kindersley
A visual index of root vegetables.
Below the watercolour painting
is a highly finished sepia line
drawing to comply with the
brief that there should be strong
evidence of drawing to support
the ethnic feel of the book.

147
BRIAN FROUD
Title: A Leprechaun
Art Director: David Larkin

Client: Peacock Press/
Harry Abrams
An illustration from *Faeries*.

148
ALAN LEE
Title: Boggarts Mining
An illustration from *Faeries*.

149
PHILIP HOOD
Art Director: Mike Spiller
Client: McClean Hunter
The painting of the legs of a man
in a deck chair drawing the graph
in the sand formed the cover of
Business Systems and Equipment.

150,151
CAROL BINCH
Title: Tough Trip Through
Paradise (top)
Art Director: Ken Sims
Client: Sphere Books

Title: Belinda
Art Director: John Munday
Client: Transworld
Publishers Ltd.

152
PENELOPE JANE WURR
Title: King in the Bath (top)
The Library (below)
Two illustrations from the book
The Hall of Greenfingers, which
the artist is writing. Media:
Gouache, watercolour and
crayon.

153
GORDON CRABB
Title: The Watsons (right)
Art Director: John Munday
Client: Transworld
Publications Ltd.
Painted in oils on watercolour
board. The underpainting is in a
mixture of watercolours, gouache
and acrylic paints, sealed with
an acrylic medium.

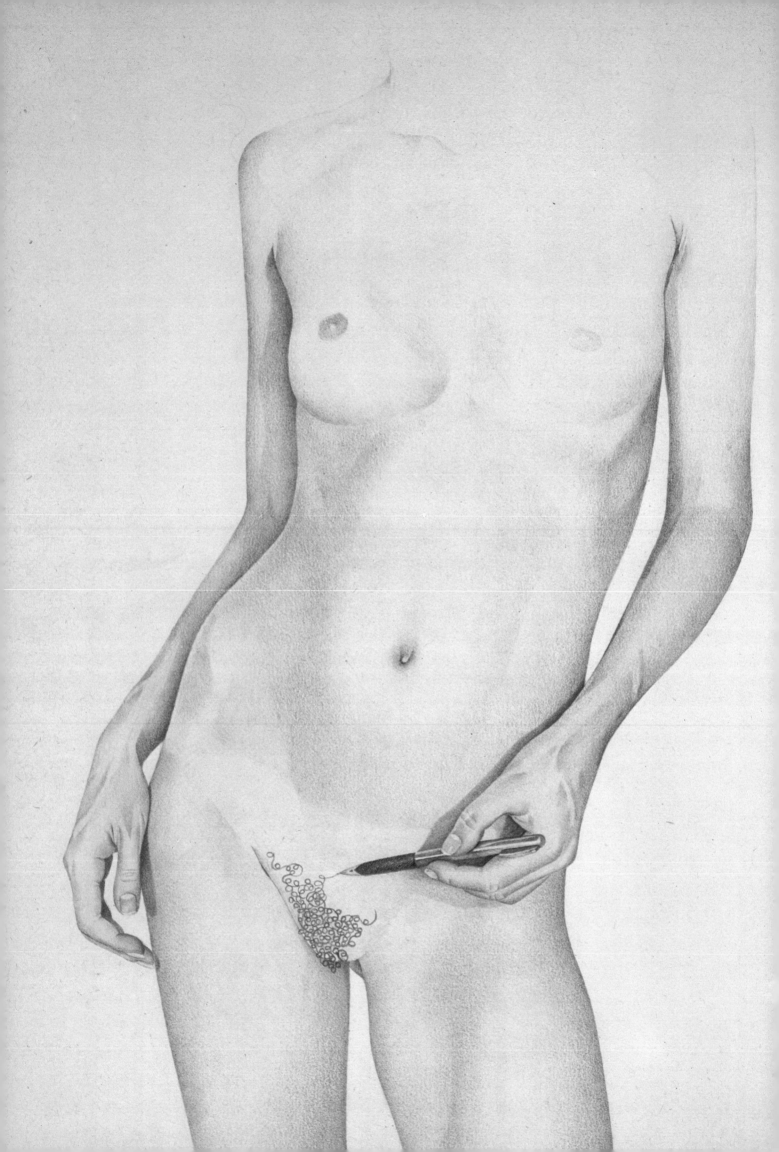

154
CLAIRE DAVIES
Title: Sexual Signatures (left)
Art Director: Ken Simms
Client: Sphere Books

155
ANNE YVONNE GILBERT
Title: Linden and Zoe (above)
This is one from a series of
coloured pencil drawings of two
friends which were produced as
sample pieces for the artist's
portfolio.

156
SALLY LAUNDER
Title: Bliss
Art Director: Cherriwyn Magill
Client: Macmillan & Co. Ltd.
The design for a book jacket was
done in watercolour. The size of
the original is 230 mm x 370 mm.

157,158
KEN LAIDLAW
Title: The Emerald Peacock
(above)
Art Director: David K Jones
Client: Woman's Realm
A full-colour page illustration
for Part Two of the serialised
story of the same name by
Katherine Gordon.
Title: Flavours of Spain (left)
Art Director: Anne Davison
Client: Cassell & Collier
Macmillan
A book jacket illustration.

159
KEN THOMPSON
Title: Cream Cheese (right)
Art Director: Ken Thompson
Client: Chris Meiklejohn
An illustration for inclusion in
a promotional book.

160
PETER WARNER
Title: Tawny Owl—Study
The artist found the owl shortly
after it had been killed by a car.
He sought to record the bird's
beauty before it withered.
Medium: Watercolour. Original
size: 22" x 18".

161
JOHN THOMPSON-
STEINKRAUSS
Title: Rabbit
Self-promotional illustration
drawn to a brief on 'Hazel' in
Watership Down. The original is
life size and was done using
acrylic and gouache.

162
MATTHEW HILLIER
Title: Goldcrest
Art Director: David Roberts
Client: Guinness
Superlatives Ltd.
Britain's smallest bird, the
Goldcrest (male) was drawn by
the artist for the 1978 Guinness
Book of Records. Medium:
Gouache. Original size: 14" x 10."

163, 164
CECIL VIEWEG
Title: All The Day Long (top)
Time And The Hour (above)
Art Director: Mike Dempsey
Client: Fontana

165
CECIL VIEWEG
Title: Crossfire Trail (top)
Art Director: Dave Rodi
Client: Tandem Books/
W H Allen

166
GORDON CRABB
Title: Crimson Creek
Art Director: Mike Dempsey
Client: Fontana
The artist wanted to avoid
typical western painting colours
and the fashionable perception
of that genre and period. The
painting is in oils on watercolour board.

167
PETER RICHARDSON
Title: Through the
Looking Glass
Art Director: Clare Osborn
Client: Pan Books
The cover illustration for a
paperback edition of the well-
known tale by Lewis Carroll.

168
ALAN LEE
Title: Hist Whist
Art Director: Delia Delderfield
Client: Pan Books

169, 170
PAUL WRIGHT
Title: The Pierhead Jump (top)
Art Director: Cherriwyn Magill
Client: Macmillan & Co. Ltd.
Title: Ramage's Diamond (right)
Art Director: Mike Dempsey
Client: Fontana Books

171
GEOFF HUNT
Title: The Lonely Sea And
The Sky (top)
Art Director: David Larkin
Client: Pan Books

172
COLIN BACKHOUSE
Title: A Calendar of Love
Art Director: Steve Abis
Client: Granada Publishing

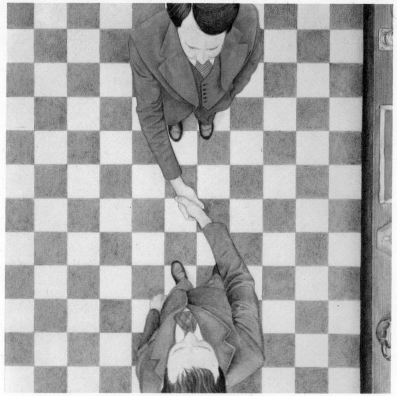

173
PETER KNOCK
Title: A Game of Consequences
Art Director: Cherriwyn Magill
Client: Macmillan & Co. Ltd.

174
CLARE HATCHER
Title: Papersnake
Art Director: Cherriwyn Magill
Client: Macmillan & Co. Ltd.
Both illustrations on this page
were commissioned for book
jackets.

175
TONY MEEUWISSEN
Title: Times Delight
Art Director: Bill Brott
Client: Hamlyn Publishing
Group
A front cover illustration for a
book of poetry for all seasons.

176
CAROL LAWSON
Title: Tiger Moth
The watercolour painting is one
of a series of illustrations for a
book on fantasy animals.

177
SYLFIA ELLEN WILLIAMS
Title: Froggy Went A Courting
Media: Watercolour and crayon
on paper
Original size: 8¾" x 8¾."

178
GWEN FULTON
Title: Owl And The Pussycat
Art Director: Ian Craig
Client: Jonathan Cape Ltd.
An illustration from the book of
the same name by Edward Lear,
to accompany the verse 'They
dine on mince, and slices of
quince which they ate with a
runcible spoon.'

179
PETER CHURCH
Title: The Garden

180
TONY ROBERTS
Title: A World Out Of Time
Art Director: Pat Mortemore
Client: Futura Publications
A wrap-around jacket executed
in gouache on board.
Original size: 22″ x 15¾″

181
SUSIE LACOME
Art Director: David Sim
Client: Cannongate Publishing
A full-colour illustration for
the children's story *Princess
Pruneface*.

182
TONY McSWEENEY
Title: The Pit And The
Pendulum (above)
One of a series of illustrations to
The Works of Edgar Allan Poe.
Media: Watercolour and pencil.
Original size: 85mm x 102mm.
Title: The New Woman and
The Victorian Novel
Art Director: Cherriwyn Magill
Client: Macmillan *& Co.* Ltd.
A personal interpretation of an
1894 *Punch* cartoon.
Media: Watercolour, gouache
and pencil.
Original size: 210mm x 330mm.

183
ANGELA BARRETT
Title: Nausea
Six from a series of 11 illustrations
for *Nausea* by Jean-Paul Sartre.
10 cm x 11 cm. Ink and watercolour on board. The drawings
were done when the artist was
a final-year student.

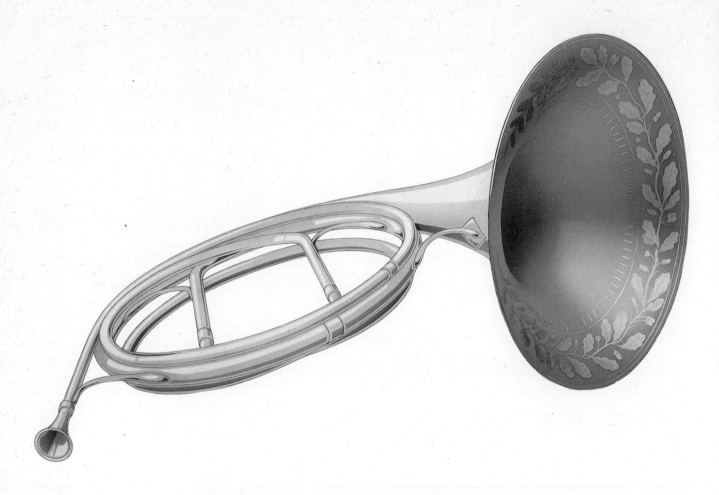

184
DAVID PENNY
Title: French Horn (top)
Client: Allen, Penny Ltd.
A colour illustration for a
dummy book.
Media: Watercolour on line
board.
Title: Wooden Wheels
Client: Mitchell Beazley Ltd.
A colour illustration for the
International Book of Wood.
Media: Watercolour on fashion
board.

185
PETER MORTER
Title: Fish and Shellfish
Art Director: Sue Casebourne
Client: Mitchell Beazley Ltd.
The reference for the water-
colour still life was taken fresh
from the fishmonger's slab.

186
GRAHAM SMITH
Title: Chartres Cathedral
Art Director: Andrew Lawson
Client: Elsevier International
Projects Ltd.
A reconstruction of a cross-
section of the cathedral to
illustrate a section of a book on
Gothic architecture called
Guide to Architecture by
Stephen Gardiner.

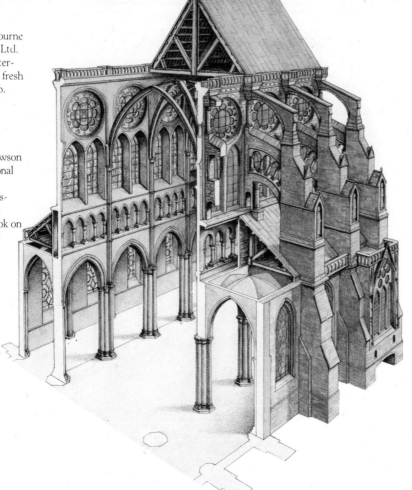

187
ROBIN JACQUES
Title: A book of Marvels
and Magic
Editor: Barbara Leach
Client: Methuen and Co.
The two drawings are from a
book of the same title which is
the most recent of 17 by the
same author and illustrator.

188
LYNETTE HEMMANT
Title: The Dancing Bear
Art Director: Robert Aspinall
Client: The Windmill Press
The ink and watercolour
drawing illustrates a poem of the
same name by Rachel Field.

189
TERENCE DALLEY
Title: St Mary the Virgin and
Putney Bridge
Client: The Putney Society
One of seven drawings from
Putney, A Brief History.

190
LYNNE BURNES
Title: A Kindle Of Kittens
Art Director: Marni Hodgkin
Client: Macmillan & Co. Ltd.
A colour specimen done for a
new book by Rumen Gouden to
be published by Macmillan.

191
PETER CHURCH
Title: Alice
This specimen illustration was
completed in pen and ink, and
the original size was 12″ x 13″.
The artist tried to achieve the
effect of the sentimental style of
tapestry popular in the
Victorian era.

192
MICHAEL HESLOP
Title: Silver On The Tree
Art Director: Jane Burkett
Client: Chatto and Windus
The illustration is a composite
of the elements within the story.

193
PETER GOODFELLOW
Title: Jesus Died in Kashmir
Art Director: Ken Sims
Client: Sphere Books

194
PETER BROOKES
Title: Regional and
Urban Economy
Art Director: David Pelham
Client: Penguin Books

195
PHILLIDA GILI
Title: Archie Goes To Chapel
(above left and right)
Art Director: Jonathan Gili
Client: John Murray
The illustration was done in
watercolour, was 4⅜"x 6" and
was based on a visit to the
village mentioned in the book
Archie and the Strict Baptists.

196
JENNY POWELL
Title: Girl with Cottage (right)
This experimental, unpublished
drawing was done in conte
pencil and watercolour on an
emulsion base. The original size
was 14"x 9"

197
JANNAT MESSENGER
Title: Miss Read's Country
Companion (right)
Art Director: Ivan Holmes
Client: Penguin Books Ltd.
The illustration was produced
for the boxed edition of several
titles. It was done with water-
colour on Fabriano paper and
the original size is
194 mm x 299 mm.

198
CHRIS WINN
Untitled
The drawing is from an
unpublished children's story

*The Island and the Big White
Lump,* which was written by
the artist. Medium: Coloured
pencils.

199
NITA SOWTER
Title: Rainbow's People At Work
Art Director: Ian Craig
Client: Jackdaw
The brief was to provide an
alphabet of people at work to
the original size 17″ x 10″. Media:
Ink and coloured pencils.

200
RAY SMITH
Title: 'Ah! Fresh air,' said Barley
Art Director: Anthony Colwell
Client: Jonathan Cape Ltd.

An illustration from *The Long Dive*, painted in acrylic colours

201
RON SANDFORD
Title: Medieval Months
Art Director: Ken Brooks
Client: The Longman Group
A two-page illustration for

Picture of the Past, 2, a history course for secondary schools.

202
PETER GREGORY
Title: ESA Space Shuttle
Art Director: Anita Townsend
Client: Grisewood and Dempsey
The full-colour artwork was
executed in ink, and was one of
a number of illustrations based
on NASA drawings for a
children's educational book.

203
COLIN HAWKINS
Title: Weight Problems At
Speed of Light
Art Director:
Jacqueline Cowdrey
Client: Theorem Publishing Ltd.
The artist was asked to illus-
trate the theory that a space
traveller's weight would increase
enormously approaching the
speed of light. Media: Ink on line
board. Original size:
130 mm x 105 mm.

204
PETER MORTER
Title: Baroque Organ
Art Director: Nick Edison
Client: Harrow House Editions
The artist's research was done
in the organ builder's workshop.
Many preliminary sketches and
measured drawings were made.

205
MARY RAYNER
Title: A Face Smiled Fondly
Down At Garth
Art Director: Marni Hodgkin
Client: Macmillan & Co. Ltd.
One of 27 illustrations done in
pen, watercolour and poster
paint for a book written by
the artist.

206
LOUISE VOCE
Title: The Cat That Walked
By Himself (above)
An illustration for the Rudyard
Kipling story of the same title.
Media: Watercolour and ink.
Original size: 4¼" x 3."

207
CHERYL ASHE
Title: Frustration (left)
The watercolour painting is an
unpublished illustration executed
as part of an experimental series
of fairy animal studies. The work
is in preparation for a children's
book to be written by the
illustrator.

208
NORMAN MESSENGER
(above right)
A watercolour and pencil
drawing for inclusion in a
promotional book published by
the artist's agent.

209
ERIC ROWE
Title: Kym (right)
Art Director: John Munday
Client: Transworld Publishers
Ltd.
An illustration for the cover of
the cat's 'autobiography'.

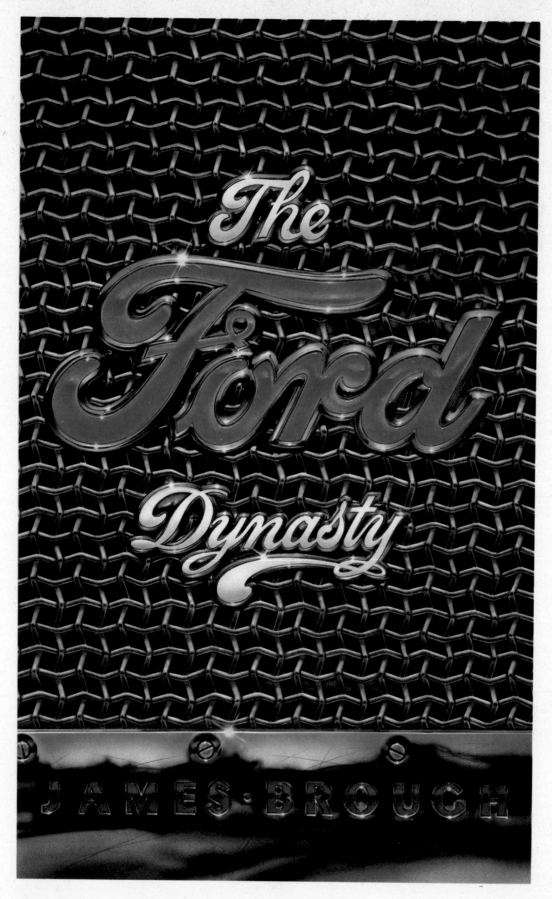

210
CHRIS MOORE
Title: The Ford Dynasty
Art Director: Nick Thirkell
Client: W H Allen

211
ANDREW HOLMES
Title: Big Rigs
Art Director: Bob Morley
Client: Quarto Publishing Ltd.
The cover illustration for a book
on American trucks and truckers.

212
BRIAN SANDERS
Title: A Day in the Life of
Ivan Denisovitch

213
ANTHONY KERINS
Title: Germinal

214, 215
STEPHEN CARTWRIGHT
Title: Saturday Night (left)
Dancing Lesson (above)

216, 217
KEVIN O'KEEFE
Title: The Misunderstanding
(above)
Il Paradiso (below)
Both illustrations were executed
for the artist's own use, and both
were done on board, using
technical pen, watercolour and
sprayed dyes.

218
SIMON STERN
Title: The Hobyas
Client: Methuen Children's
Books Ltd.
The artist has retold and illus-
trated this neglected folk-tale.
The Hobya's tadpole shape was
the invention of John D Batten,
who first drew them.
Medium: Gouache with line
overlay.

219
DAVID SIM
Title: Cornelius and the
Magic Cloak (top)
Art Director: Susie Lacome
A black and white illustration
to accompany the text of a
children's story which the
artist had written.

220
GERALD ROSE
Title: Lion Bit It
Art Director: Phyllis Hunt
Client: Faber and Faber Ltd.
An illustration for a
children's book.

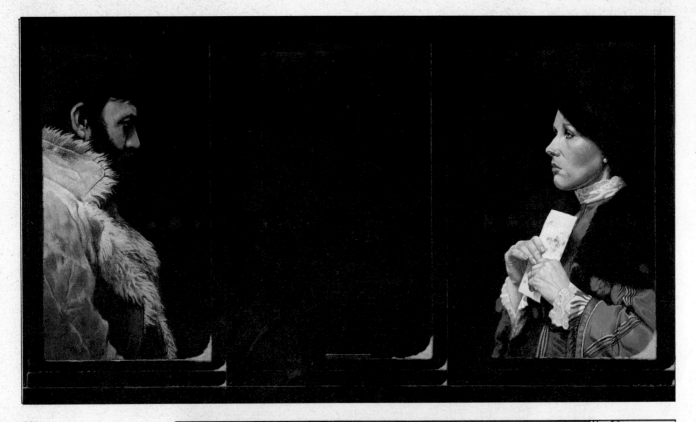

221
GEORGE SMITH
Title: Last Train to Shanghai
(above)
Art Director: John Gibbs
Client: Routledge and
Kegan Paul
A man and a woman sit opposite
one another in the train. The
artist was briefed to incorporate
the train in the painting without
creating a multiple image.

222
ERIC STEMP
Untitled (right)
Art Director: Willie Landels
Client: Harpers and Queen
Magazine
A cover illustration for the
magazine's guide to the 300 best
hotels in the world.

223
JOHN HOLDER
Title: Fall from an Ordinary
(far right)
Art Director:
Mike Graham-Cameron
Client: Dinosaur Books
National Trust
An illustration from *Cycling On*
by Ray Hallett.
Media: Pen, ink, watercolours
and CS2 board.

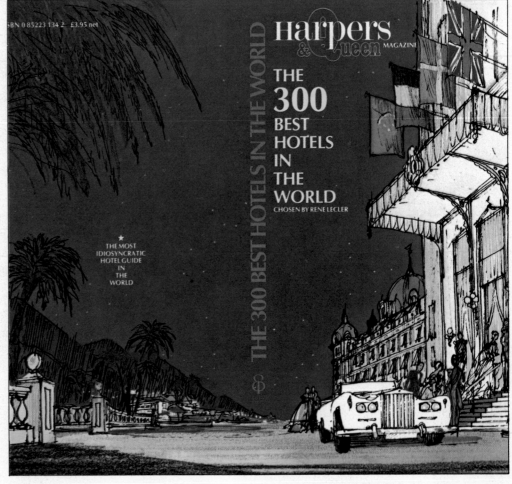

224
DAVID HOLMES
Title: Kim (above)
Art Director: David Larkin
Client: Pan Books Ltd.

225
DILWYN KNOX
Title: York Gate
Art Director: Ian Scott
Agency: Fletcher Shelton
Reynold & Dorrell Ltd.
This is one of a series of 12 wood
engravings designed as tailpieces
to the chapters of a book about
Crofts.

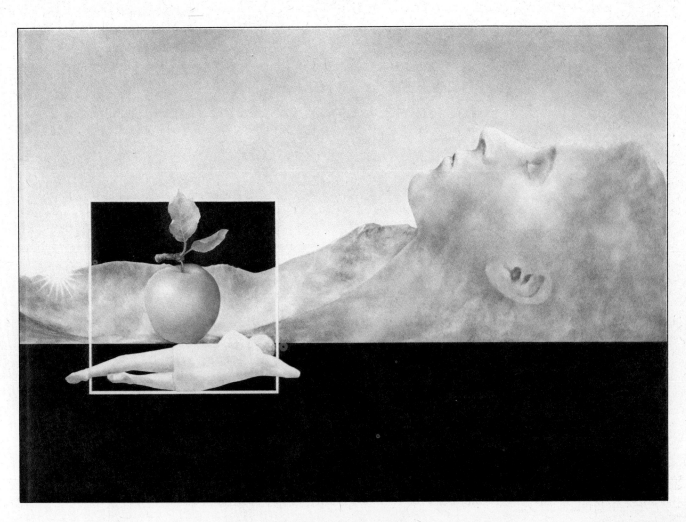

226
DAVE HOLMES
Title: Sleeping Under the Sky
(above)
Dreaming (below)

227
SARA MIDDA
Title: Come Hither Volume I
(top left)
Volume II (top right)
Art Director: Treld Bicknell
Client: Kestrel Books
Watercolour paintings for book
covers for anthologies of poetry
by Walter de la Mare.

228
FRANK DICKENS
Title: Executives Under
Pressure
Art Director: Cherriwyn Magill
Client: Macmillan & Co. Ltd.

229
PENELOPE JANE WURR
Title: Teapot Chased By Birds
One of a series of illustrations
for *Teapot Tale,* a story about a
teapot with feet.

230
JIM BURNS
Title: Mechanismo (above)
Art Director: Philip Dunn
Client: Pierrot Publishing Ltd.
A book jacket based on the idea
that the book concentrates on
the mechanisms of science
fiction.
Media: Oils on acrylic-primed
line board.

231
TIM WHITE
Title: The Day After Tomorrow
(near right)
Art Director: Tony Dominy
Client: New English Library

232
COLIN HAY
Title: Enchanted Pilgrimage
(far right)
Art Director: Mike Dempsey
Client: Fontana

233
CHRIS ACHILLEOS
Title: The Cabal
(opposite above)
Art Director: John Munday
Client: Transworld
Publishers Ltd.

234
DAVID ROE
Title: Dragonsong
(opposite below)
Art Director: John Munday
Client: Transworld
Publishers Ltd.
A design for a book jacket that
was also used as a poster
promoting the book.

235
JENNIFER EACHUS
Title: Johnny Goodlooks
Art Director: Peter Bennett
Client: Associated Book
Publishers.

236
ALLAN MANHAM
Title: Saville
Art Director: Ivan Holmes
Client: Penguin Books
David Storey's novel tells of the
life of a young boy in a mining
village. The illustration was
painted in acrylic on canvas and
the original measures 11" x 17".

237
JAMES MARSH
Title: Anthem II
Art Director: Jill Mumford
Client: Polydor Records
An illustration of a violin piece
by the pop group The Sweet.

PRINT AND DESIGN

238 239
DAVID LEAKE
Title: The Case of the Bent
Policeman (top)
Signs of the Zodiac:
Libra
The illustration of the policeman
was done with gouache and an
airbrush, while the Libra sign
was done in ink and watercolour
with an airbrush.

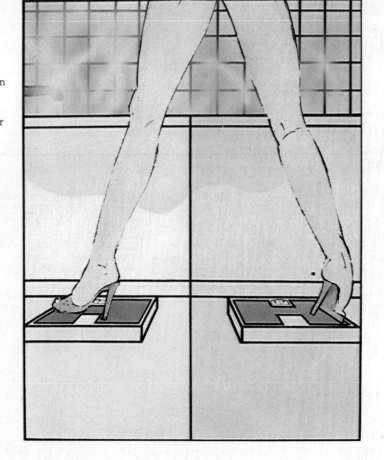

240
RICHARD DEVEREUX
Title: Cherry Cake
An experimental illustration
done with Caran d'Ache crayon
on Ivory board.

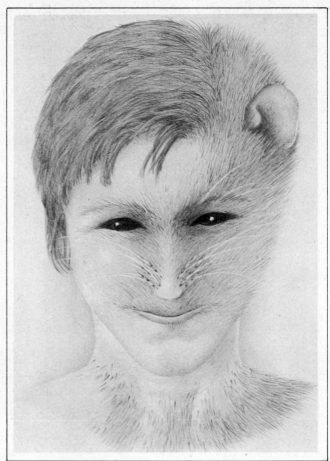

241
JULIAN GRADDON
Title: Jean Cocteau
Client: Mark Ramon
The drawing done in brown
crayon was for a poster on
The Genius of Cocteau.

242
ANN SOUTHWARD
Title: Self-portrait as a Rat
(above right)

243
MIK BROWN
Title: Ebeneezer Mooge
Art Director: David Costa
Client: Rocket Records
The design for a record cover
shows an old man playing a
steam 'mooge'.

244
JOHN THIRSK
Title: Wheelwright
Art Director: Tony Ward, Graffiti
Client: Esso Petroleum Co
One of 12 drawings for the
Esso craftsmen calendar.
Pen and watercolour.

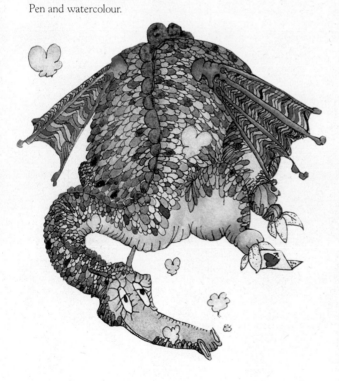

245
ANGIE SAGE
Title: Valentine Dragon
The design is one of six dragon
greetings cards which cover a
variety of occasions. They were
completed while the artist was a
student and were done with
watercolour and Indian ink.

246
WENDY DOWSON
Title: Cusworth Village
A sewn picture of the village in
South Yorkshire. Original size:
28" x 22"

PHILLIP GOODHAND-TAIT
TEACHING AN OLD DOG NEW TRICKS

247
MIKE NOOME
Title: Teaching An Old Dog
New Tricks
Art Director: Peter Wagg
Client: Chrysalis Records
The brief was to move away from
the traditional photographic
image of the solo artist and to
treat the subject with warmth
and humour.
Media: Airbrush and gouache.

CHR 1146

Side 1
AIRBORNE
THE LADY LIVES IN ENGLAND
ARE YOU ALONE?
PRIVATE LIVES
JUST A DREAM

Side 2
PARADE
ANGELTOWN
DON'T TREAT YOUR LOVER LIKE A THIEF
I WANT TO WINTER WITH YOU
IF WE EVER MEET AGAIN

All songs written and composed by Phillip Goodhand-Tait
Produced by Muff Winwood

Chrysalis
Chrysalis Records Limited, 388-396 Oxford Street, London W1N 9HE.

248, 249
RODERICK ELLIS
Title: I Think A Zebra Would
Be The Best Pet to Have
A large pencil drawing
depicting a zebra-skin sofa.
Title: If I Had A Snake For A
Pet…
The second of two illustrations
based on the poem *Ménagerie a
Deux*. Both of these drawings
take the theme of natural,
animal elements existing in a
synthetic environment in rela-
tion to the human element.

250
LJILJANA RYLANDS
Title: Lion (top)
Tiger (above)
Art Director: Jan Pienkovski
Client: Gallery Five Ltd
Both designs are for greetings
cards, and are hand embroidered
on canvas. The brief required
only that designs should be
embroidered and that the format
should be square.

251
SARA MIDDA
Title: Some People Love
Cats... (left)
Bicycle (right)
The Love of Cats illustration is
a black-and-white line drawing.
The Bicycle is an etching.

252
PETER GREGORY
Title: The Queen of Scots
Art Director: Peter Jordan
Client: Spastics Society
A full colour illustration
executed in ink for the Society's
Christmas stamp.

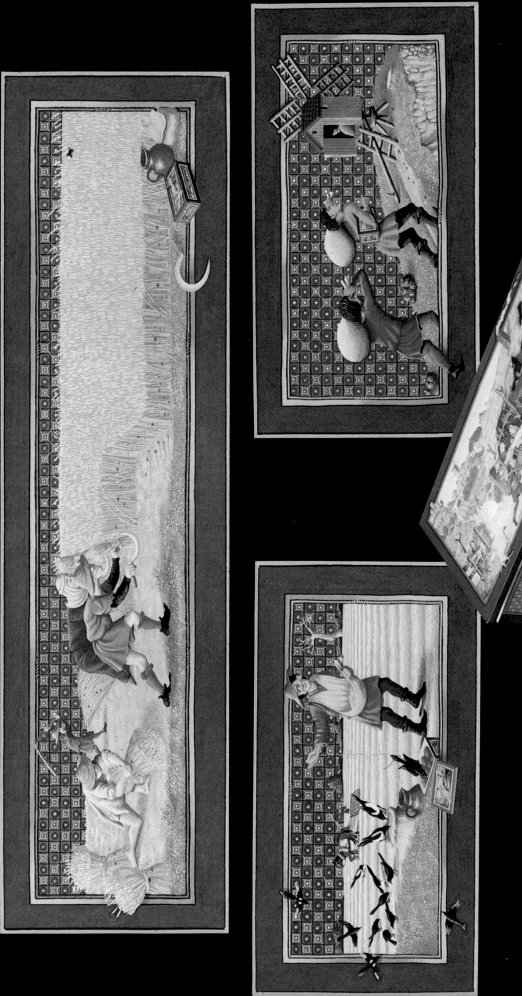

253
PETER BROOKES
Art Director: Peter Windette
Client: Crabtree and
Evelyn Limited
The illustrations were

lid of a tin for biscuits from the
Yorkshire Dales. The drawings
were medieval in style in order
to suggest the hand-made, rustic

LOVE IS LIKE OXYGEN | You get too much you get too high | No

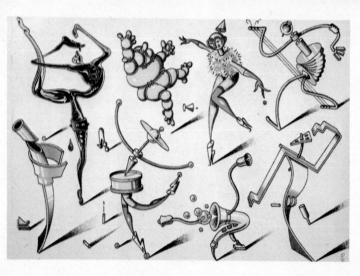

254
BUSH HOLLYHEAD
Title: Love Is Like
Oxygen (above)
Art Director: Jill Mumford
Client: Polydor Records
One of a number of illustrations
of songs by the group The Sweet
for a calendar.
Title: A Party (left)
Art Director: Bush Hollyhead
Client: NTA Studios
Design for a party invitation.

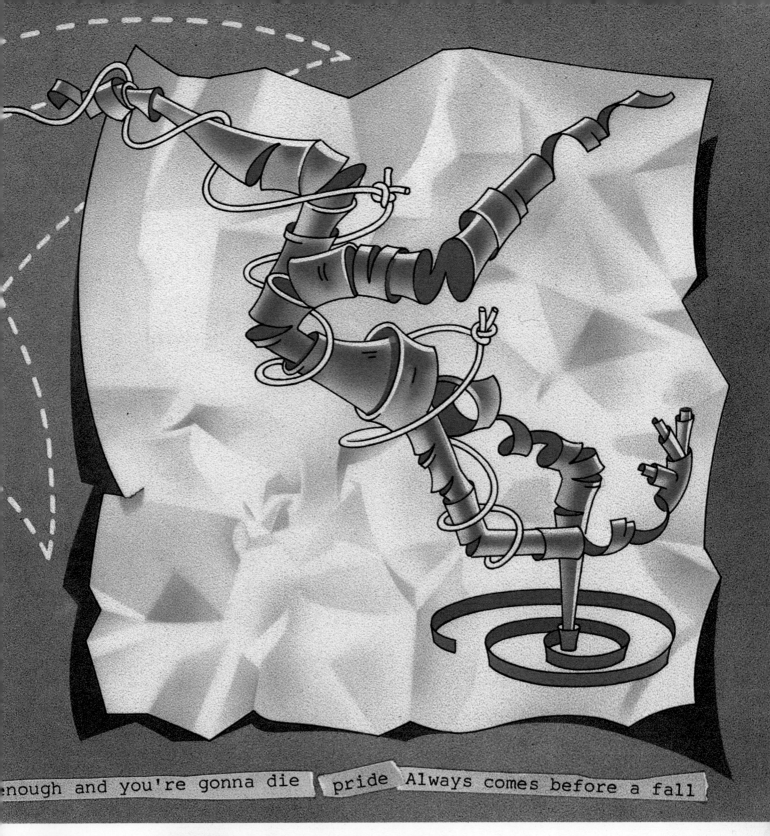

enough and you're gonna die | pride | Always comes before a fall

255
GEORGE RUSSELL
Title: Five Crises of Life

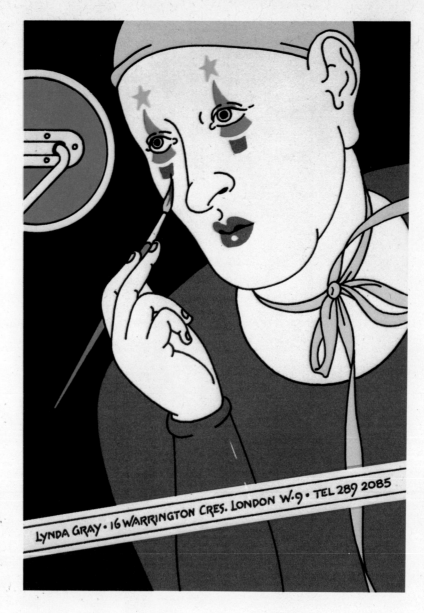

LYNDA GRAY • 16 WARRINGTON CRES. LONDON W·9 • TEL 289 2085

256
LYNDA GRAY
Title: Christmas Card
The card was done for the
artist's own use.
Medium: Gouache.

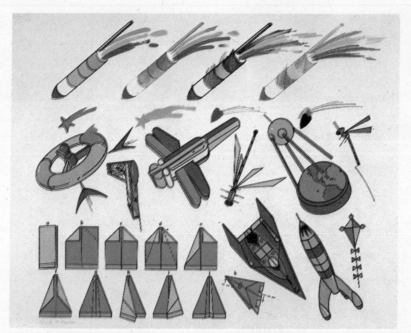

257
CHRIS McEWAN
Title: Flyers

258
BUSH HOLLYHEAD
Title: The Music (top right)
The Rehearsal (right)
Art Director: Storm Thorgenson,
Hipgnosis
Client: Emka Productions Ltd
Two of a series of drawings on
dogs, pigs and sheep for 'Pink
Floyd Animals' sheet music.

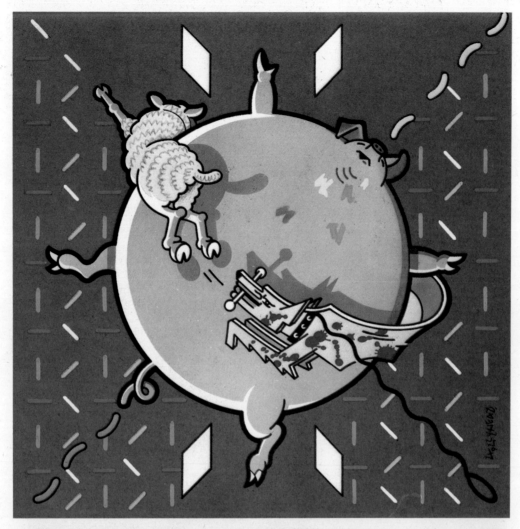

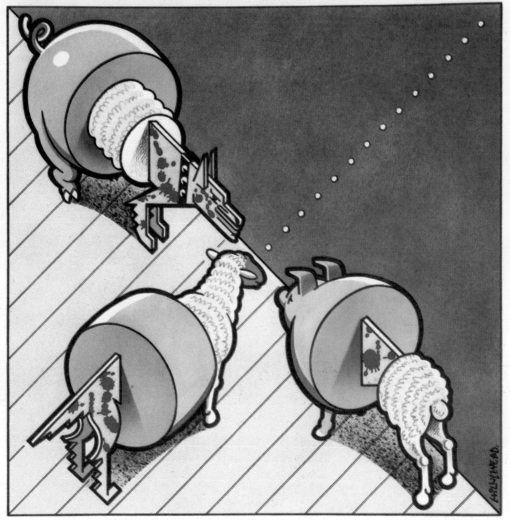

259
BOB NORRINGTON
Title: October—Rita Hayworth
An illustration for one month of
the birth dates of movie stars.
Media: Gouache, poster colour
on line board.

260
DOUG HARKER
Title: Soccer All Stars
Art Director: Mitch Walker,
J Walter Thompson Co Ltd

Client: Golden Wonder Limited
The artist was commissioned to
produce drawings of football
stars for 24 cards.

261
BRIAN SANDERS
Title: James Herriot Calendar
Art Director: David Larkin
Client: Peacock Press
The artist was briefed to produce
twelve full-colour illustrations
for the second Herriot calendar.
The illustrations shown here
are for July (above), May (above
right), and June (right), and were
executed in watercolour on
rough paper.

262
TERRY DOWLING
Title: Tiger Man And Woman
Client: Mappin Art Gallery,
Sheffield
An illustration from the story
Tigers which was reproduced as
the introduction to a self-
promotional catalogue for a one
man exhibition.
Media: Pen and ink.
Original size: 14cm x 17.6cm.

263
JOHN WOODCOCK
Title: Cat
This illustration was conceived
as a self-promotion exercise, and
as an experiment in the use of
watercolour as a medium for
detailed painting.
Title: Irish Setter (below).

264

ERIC TENNEY
Title: Snow Leopard (top)
Art Director: Suzy Lewis
Client: Jenks Bros Foods Ltd
One of four prints of big cats to
be used as promotional material
for Purina cat food.

Title: Watership Down Calendar
Art Director: David Larkin
Client: Avon Books Ltd
The rabbit sitting on a hillock
in sunset formed part of a
calendar arising out of the book
Watership Down.

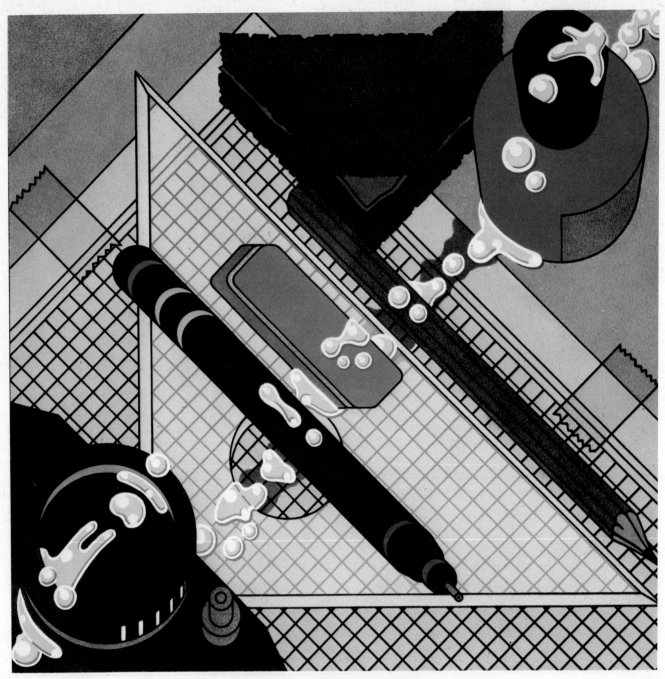

265, 266, 267, 268
GEORGE HARDIE
Title: Walk Away René (top left)
Art Director: Storm Thorgerson,
Hipgnosis
Client: Dragon's World Ltd
A back cover of a book about
the work of some designers
and photographers.

Title: History. The Beatles
Break Up (top right)
Art Director: Storm Thorgerson,
Hipgnosis
Client: Thames Television
An illustration of the break-up
of the pop group The Beatles.

Title: A Menu Illustration
(far right)
Client: A private dining club

Christmas Card
Art Director: John Gorham
Client: John Sherfields
Studio Ltd.

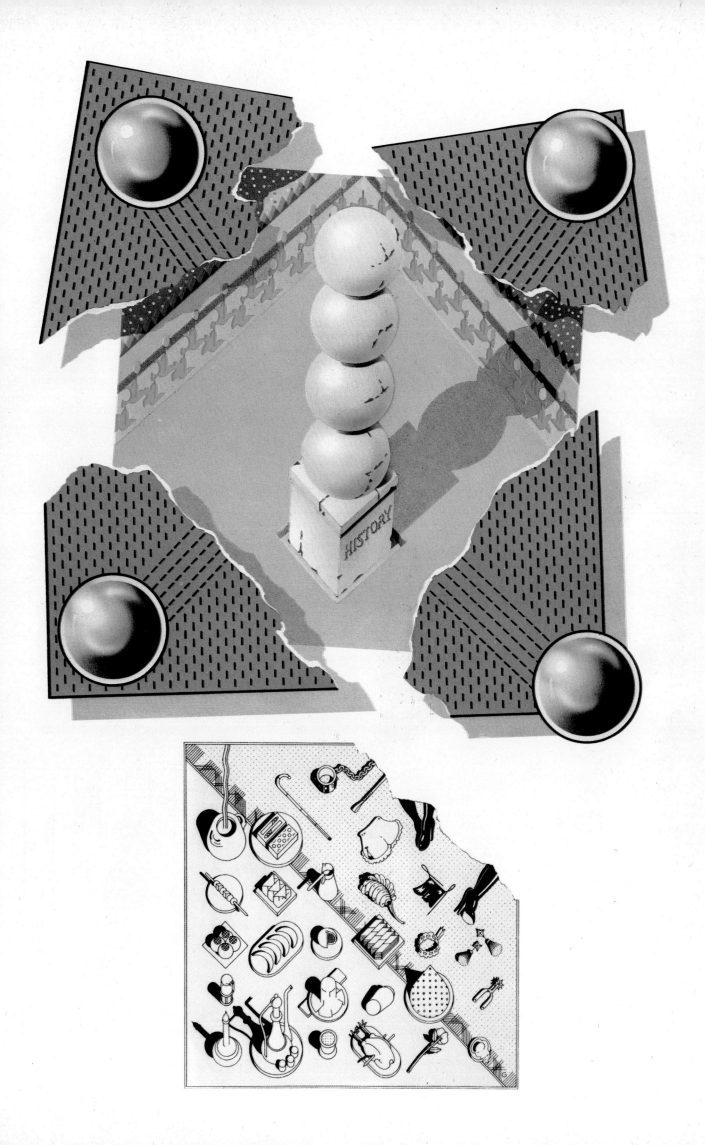

HISTORY

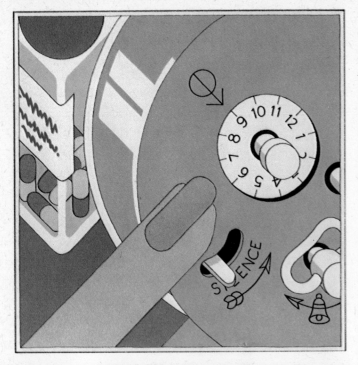

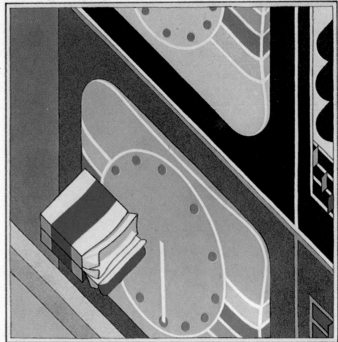

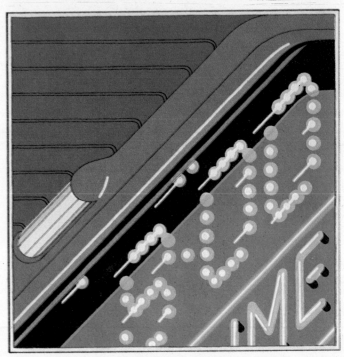

269
GEORGE HARDIE
Title: Clocks
Art Director: Aubrey Powell,
Hipgnosis
Client: McCartney
Productions Ltd
The drawings were used for
chapter headings in a book of
photographs of The Wings tour
of America. The book was
divided into eight chapters
based on particular hours of
the day.

270
GEORGE HARDIE
Title: One Second Later
Client: Mel Calman,
The Workshop
An illustration done for an
exhibition of pictures of cats.

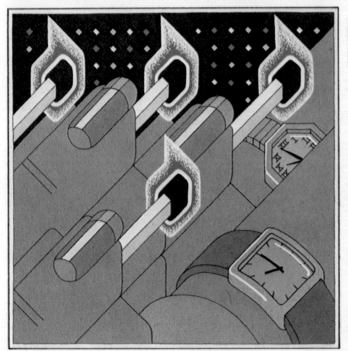

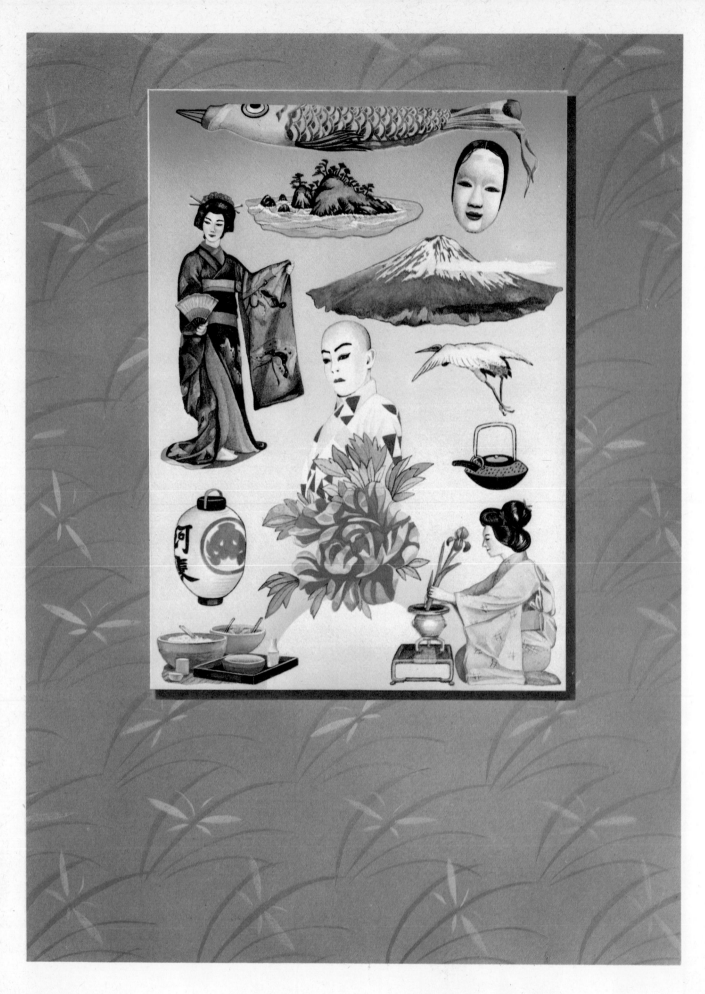

271
HELEN COWCHER
Title: Japan
An unpublished work forming
one page of a calendar.

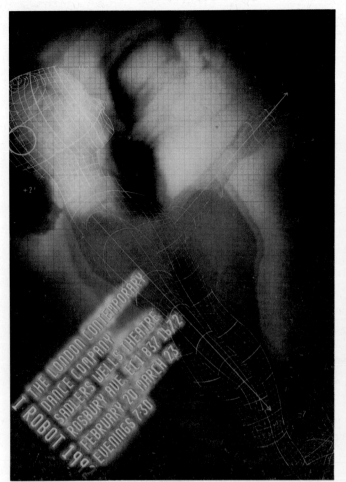

272 , 273, 274
ALWYN CLAYDEN
Title: 1 Robot 1992 (top left)
There'll Always Be An England
(top right)
Is There Life On Mars? (above)
All three illustrations were
done while the artist was a
student for college projects.

275
LIZ MOYES
Title: For Julie and Edward
A portrait of the sons of friends
of the artist. Done on water-
colourboard in watercolour.

276
MIKE TREVITHICK
Title: Pavement Cat
A black-and-white line cut of a
cat on a pavement.

277
LIZ MOYES
Title: For Cynthia
A portrait of a girl against a
fabric background. A friend
whose main interest is needle-
work commissioned this painting
from the artist.

278
CAROL LAWSON
Title: Red Riding Hood (top)
Title: The Bremen Town
Musicians
Art Director: Mark Suckle
Client: Franklin Mint
International
Two of a series of twelve
illustrations to Grimm's Fairy
Tales reproduced in a limited
edition on porcelain plates.

279
JUAN WIJNGAARD
Title: Seagulls
Art Director: Jan Pienkowski
Client: Gallery Five Ltd.
One of a series of 12 drawings
showing scenes through win-
windows to be used for greetings
cards and a calendar.

280
TERRY PASCOE
Title: Aubrey Littlejohn—
Gentleman
Art Director: Terry Pascoe
Client: Rainyday Postcards
One of a series of postcards
based on Cornish folklore. The
work reflects the artist's interest
in Elizabethan miniatures.
Media: Ballpoint, watercolour
and crayon.
Original size: 12″ x 9½″

281
DAVE HOPKINS
Title: Butcher (above)
Art Director: John Rogers
Client: Pran & Torgesen
The work was executed for the decoration of a liver paté tin.

Title: Wheel of Fortune (right)
Art Director: Paul Humphries
Client: Black Cat Cigarettes
An illustration for a cigarette card album.

282
ROBIN BUSFIELD
Title: Angelique
A self-promotional work executed in watercolours with an airbrush. The illustration was eventually used for printed fabric and wallpaper.

283
PETER TILL
Title: Situational Phobias
Art Director: Major Steadman,
Dragon Productions
Client: Geigy Pharmaceuticals
This is one of four background
illustrations for a film on phobias.

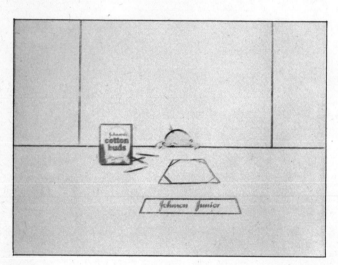

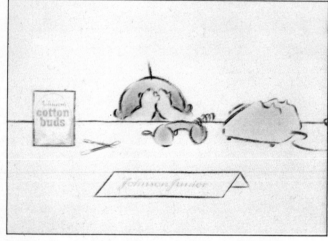

284
PAUL DAVIES
Title: Promotionally Punch
Drunk Milkie (top left)
The brief was to illustrate the
phrase which forms the title. The
cartoon, done in Magic Marker
and pencil, was used in a presentation for Unigate Dairies
by the advertising agency.

285
KEITH S ALDRED
Title: Untamed World (top right)
Art Director: Keith S Aldred
Client: Granada Television
The osprey's head is one of a
series of British Birds of Prey
which the artists drew at
Manchester Museum. It is about
4" across, painted in inks, and
forms part of a promotion for a
television programme of the
same title.

286, 287
RUSSELL HALL
Title: Button Cods (centre left)
Mums (centre right)
Art Director: Rod Howick,
Richard Williams Animation
Client: Johnson & Johnson Ltd.
Two frames each from 30-second
television commercials. The
cartoon character, drawn in
pencil and crayon, was used for
selling a baby product for adult
usage.

288
ANNA FARRAR
Title: The Old Woman Who
Lived in a Shoe (above)
Art Director: Anna Farrar
Client: Granada Television
The first of two illustrations for
the children's programme A
Handful of Songs. Drawn with
pen, coloured pencils and inks.
19" x 25".

289
ANNA FARRAR
Title: Come Back Little Sheba
Art Director: Anna Farrar
Client: Granada Television
The illustrations are sections of a
roller caption 12″ deep x 9′ in
length, across which the camera
pans. They were used as titles for
Come Back Little Sheba and were
to evoke the atmosphere of small-
town America in the 1950's.
Media: Pen and ink with
coloured washes.

290
JOHN LEECH
Title: Hard Times
Art Director: Philip Buckley
Client: Granada Television
The illustration was part
of the title for the television
drama series *Hard Times*.

291
ALEX FORBES
Title: The Last Round (above)
Client: Thames Television
A promotional trailer shown
between television programmes.
Media: Watercolour, letrafilm
and wood.
Original size: 12″ x 10″.

292
ROB PAGE
Title: Rumpole of the Bailey
Art Director: Rob Page
Client: Thames Television
The illustration was for
the opening title of a television
drama series starring
Leo McKern.
Media: Coloured pencils, inks
and gouache.
Original size: 12″ x 10″.

INDEX

A

Achilleos, C. (233),
Transworld Publishers Ltd.,
61/63 Uxbridge Road,
London W5 5SA. 01-579 2652.

Aldred, Keith S. (285),
8 Redstone Road, Burnage,
Manchester 3.

Anderson, Wayne (19),
c/o Andy Archer Associates,
10 Glentworth Street,
London NW2. 01-787 3425.

Ashe, Cheryl (207),
4 Princes Avenue, Crosby,
Merseyside L23 5RR. 051-924 2571.

Austin, Alan (28), 'Courtyard',
6a Smith Street, London SW3.
01-740 2363.

B

Backhouse, Colin (172),
c/o Young Artists,
25 St. Pancras Way, London NW1.
01-387 2516.

Baines, Alan (58), 19 Willmer Road,
Anfield, Liverpool L4 2TA.
051-264 7203.

Barrett, Angela (183),
126 Alma Avenue, Hornchurch,
Essex. Hornchurch 40897.

Bell, Edward (65),
284 Earls Court Road, London SW5.
01-373 2397.

Bellinger, Trudie-Jane (41),
43 London Road, Rainham,
Gillingham, Kent. 0634 37816.

Binch, Carole (150,151),
c/o Transworld Publishers Ltd.,
61/63 Uxbridge Road,
London W5 5SA. 01-579 2652.

Bodek, Stuart (11),
Artist Partners Limited,
14-18 Ham Yard,
London W1. 01-734 7991.

Brookes, Peter (52,68,70,120,121,
122,140,194,253), 30 Vanburgh Hill,
London SE3 7UF. 01-858 9022.

Brown, Mik (243),
41 Hastings Road, Maidstone,
Kent. 678 391.

Brownfield, Mick (29,44,123,124,
125), 41 The Vineyard, Richmond,
Surrey.

Burns, Jim (230), c/o Young Artists,
25 St. Pancras Way, London NW1.
01-387 2516.

Burnes, Lynne (190),
c/o John Martin and Artists Ltd.,
5 Wardour Street,
London W1V 3HE. 01-734 9000.

Busfield, Robin (282),
5 Birch Terrace, Hanley,
Stoke-on-Trent.
Stoke-on-Trent 20544.

Butler, John (42), 3 Carlisle Street,
London W1. 01-734 6196.

C

Cartwright, Stephen (214,215),
22 White Hart Lane, Barnes,
London SW13. 01-878 2886.

Cheese, Chloe (81,82),
118 Leander Road, London SW2.

Church, Peter (179,191),
15 Acacia Court, Keynsham,
Avon BS18 2RU. Keynsham 5885.

Clayden, Alwyn (272,273,274),
13 Sulgrave Road, London W6.
01-734 4464.

Cowcher, Helen (271),
17 Knollys Road, London SW16.
01-769 5697.

Crabb, Gordon (153,166),
c/o Young Artists,
25 St. Pancras Way, London NW1.
01-387 2516.

Cracknell, Alan (15),
50 Lincoln's Inn Fields,
London WC2A 3PF.

Creswell, Pamela (36),
6 Carington Street, Loughborough,
Leicester. Loughborough 67483.

D

Dalley, Terence (55,94,189),
11 Spencer Walk,
London SW15 1PL. 01-788 6796.

Davies, Claire (154), Artist Partners,
14/18 Ham Yard, London W1.
01-734 7991.

Davies, David R. (106),
6a Pant Hirgoed, Pencoed,
Mid-Glamorgan,
South Wales CF35 6YD.

Davies, Paul (284),
18 Sinclair Gardens,
London W14 0AT. 01-603 2993.

Deshayes, Manchuelle (34),
5 Rue Mornay, 75004 Paris.
Paris 271 3991.

Devereux, Richard (240),
17 Highdown Avenue, Worthing,
West Sussex. 0243 80787.

Dickens, Frank (228),
c/o Evening Standard, Shoe Lane,
London EC4. 01-353 8000.

Dobson, Phil (26), 4 Ruskin Avenue,
Kew, Richmond, Surrey.
01-876 8340.

Dowling, Terry (262),
31 Western Drive, Fenham,
Newcastle-upon-Tyne NE4 8SQ.
Newcastle-upon-Tyne 732361.

Dowson, Wendy (246), Top Flat,
41 Belgrave Gardens, London NW8.

Dubrule, Duthy (24),
61 Ladbroke Grove,
London W11 3AT. 01-727 9333.

Duff, Leo (79), 82 Cavendish Road,
London SW12 0DF. 01-675 2688.

E

Eachus, Jennifer (235),
71 Pembroke Road, London N10.

Eastbury, Dave (98),
46 Buckmans Road, West Green,
Crawley, Sussex RH11 7DR.
Crawley 21310.

Ellis, Roderick (248,249),
Department of Illustration,
Maidstone College of Art,
Maidstone, Kent.

Ellison, Pauline (17,18,76),
24 Belsize Avenue, London NW3.
01-794 8854.

F

Farrar, Anna (288,289),
169 Palatine Road, West Didsbury,
Manchester 20. 061-445 0534.

Fern, Dan (9,10,90),
112 Hazellville Road, London N19.
01-272 9727.

Forbes, Alex (291), 79 Hall Road,
Isleworth. 01-568 3384.

Frith, Michael (46),
256 Canbury Park Road,
Kingston-upon-Thames, Surrey.
01-546 4167.

Froud, Brian (147), Artist Partners,
14/18 Ham Yard, London W1.
01-734 7991.

Fulton, Gwen (178),
c/o Jonathan Cape Ltd.,
30 Bedford Square, London WC1.
01-636 5764.

G

Garrett, Jooce (47),
c/o Artist Partners Limited,
14/18 Ham Yard,
London W1V 8DE. 01-734 7991.

Geary, John (64),
2 Book Centre Mansions,
North Circular Road,
London NW10 0JD. 01-451 0054.

George, Adrian (114),
40 Westbourne Terrace, London W2.
01-262 0010.

Gilbert, Anne Yvonne (155),
2 Huskisson Street,
Liverpool L8 7LP. 051-709 2782.

Gili, Phillida (195), 28 Ifield Road,
London SW10 9AA. 01-351 1407.

Gladwell, Guy (5), Studio,
20 Harley Road, London NW3.
01-586 0987.

Goodfellow, Peter (37,110,193),
c/o Young Artists,
25 St. Pancras Way, London NW1.
01-387 2516.

Graddon, Julian (49,241),
31 King Street, London WC2.
01-240 2077.

Gray, Lynda (69,256),
16 Warrington Crescent,
London W9. 01-289 2085.

Gregory, Peter (202,252),
37 Cantley Gardens, Ilford, Essex.
01-554 5499.

Grimwood, Brian (40,96,97),
36 Wellington Street, London WC2.
01-836 0391.

H

Hadley, Colin (25),
14 Lewes Crescent,
Brighton BN2 1SH. 0273 65195.

Hants, Harry (35), Artist Partners,
14/18 Ham Yard, London W1.
01-734 7991.

Hall, Russell (286,287),
Richard Williams Animation,
13 Soho Square, London W1.
01-437 4455.

Hardcastle, Nicholas (54,57),
Maidstone College of Art,
Maidstone, Kent.
Maidstone 57286.

Hardie, George (113,115,265,266,
267,268,269,270), NTA Studios,
44 Earlham Street, London WC2.
01-240 2779.

Harker, Doug (260),
Artist Partners Ltd.,
14/18 Ham Yard, London W1.
01-734 7991.

Hatcher, Clare (174),
1 Kingsdowne Road, Epsom,
Surrey. 78 25886.

Hawkins, Colin (203),
27 Westgrove Lane, Greenwich,
London SE10. 01-692 2054.

Hay, Colin (232), c/o Young Artists,
25 St. Pancras Way, London NW1.
01-387 2516.

Hemmant, Lynette (188),
16 Roseneath Road, London SW11.
01-223 5027.

Henwood, Malcolm (95),
'Briarfield', Bracken Road,
Cox Green, Maidenhead,
Berks. SL6 3EF. Maidenhead 70221.

Heslop, Michael (192),
24 The Strand, Topsham, Devon.
Topsham 5952.

Higgins, Paul (21), 3 Carlisle Street,
London W1. 01-734 6196.

Hillier, Matthew (162), Fairlight,
Elmer Road, Middleton-on-Sea,
W. Sussex. Middleton-on-Sea 3252.

Holder, John (39,223),
Queen Anne Lodge, Milton,
Cambridge. 0223 860638.

Hollyhead, Bush (254,258),
NTA Studies, 44 Earlham Street,
London WC2. 01-240 2942.

Holmes, Andrew (211),
2 Ardilawn Road, London N5.
01-226 2687.

Holmes, David (27,224,226),
72 Village Way, Beckenham, Kent.
01-650 2975.

Holmes, Sally (135),
126 St. Paul's Road, Islington,
London N1. 01-226 0563.

Holt, Peter (60),
c/o Ian Fleming and Associates,
3 Carlisle Street, London W1.
01-739 6196.

Hood, Philip (149),
c/o Young Artists,
25 St. Pancras Way, London NW1.
01-387 2516.

Hopkins, Dave (281),
c/o Ian Fleming Associates,
3 Carlisle Street, London W1.
01-734 6196.

Hunt, Geoff (171),
67 Schubert Road,
London SW15 2QT. 01-870 6211.

I

Ireland, John (6),
Valery Kemp Agency,
28 Branham Road, London SW5.
01-370 6602.

J

Jacques, Robin (108,109,187),
54 Waterford Road, London SW6.
01-731 0020.

Jones, Peter Andrew (143,144,145),
The Garden Flat, 756 Fulham Road,
London SW6 5SH. 01-734 2497.

K

Kerins, Anthony (66,213,239),
99 Casewick Road, West Norwood,
London SE27. 01-761 0814.

Knipe, Roy (38),
c/o Spectron Artists Ltd.,
5 Dryden Street, London WC2.
01-240 2430.

Knock, Peter (71,72,173),
52 Westbourne Grove,
Westcliff-on-Sea, Essex SS0 9TQ.

Knox, Dilwyn (225),
38b Linden Gardens,
London W2 4ER. 01-229 7800.

Lacombe, Susie (181),
26 Evelyn Gardens, London SW7.
01-373 5875.

Laidlow, Ken (157,158),
135 Graham Street, London NW1.
01-837 8606.

Launder, Sally (156), 9 Cross Street,
London SW13. 01-878 4295.

Lawson, Carol (176,278),
71 Hollingbury Park Avenue,
Brighton BN1 7JQ. 0273 559690.

Leake, David (238),
31 Mandeville House, Rolls Road,
London SE1. 01-237 0692.

Lee, Alan (148,168),
27 Lower Street, Chagford, Devon.
06473 2372.

Leech, John (290),
10 Birchvale Drive, Romily,
Stockport, Cheshire.

Le Vasseur, Peter (20),
Artist Partners Ltd., 14 Ham Yard,
London W1. 01-734 7991.

Loan, Dorothy (136),
c/o Basement Group, Bells Court,
Off Pilgrim Street,
Newcastle-upon-Tyne.

McEwan, Chris (130,131,132,257),
71 Hollinbury Park Avenue,
Brighton, Sussex. 559690.

MacKenzie, Muriel (112),
37 Londsdale Square, London N1.
01-607 3292.

McSweeney, Tony (78,182),
25 Dudley Street, Bell Green,
Coventry CV6 7EE. 0203 81683.

Manham, Allan (236),
53 Glebe Road, London SW13.
01-876 5114.

Marsh, James (237), 16 Iveley Road,
London SW4. 01-622 9530.

Martin, Clare (103), 5 Parkway,
Ratton Manor, Eastbourne,
Sussex BN20 9DU. 0323 52852.

Mason, Robert (100,101),
91 Cloudsley Road,
London N1.
837 2939.

Meeuwissen, Tony (91,175),
10 Gate Street, Lincoln's Inn Fields,
London WC2. 01-402 1118.

Messenger, Jannat (197),
75 Wendover Court,
Chiltern Street, London W1.
01-935 6343.

Messenger, Norman (208),
c/o Chris Meiklejohn Ltd.,
31 King Street, London WC2.
01-240 2077.

Midda, Sara (77,227,251),
19 Steeles Road, London NW3.
01-586 0207.

Mills, Russell (87,88,89,116,119),
25 Toriano Cottages, London NW5.
01-267 0053.

Moore, Chris (12,142,210),
42 Brandham Road,
London SE13 5RT. 01-852 3429.

Morter, Peter (146,185,205),
128 Wood Street, Barnet,
Hertfordshire. 01-440 2154.

Moyes, Liz (275,277),
Artist Partners Limited,
14/18 Ham Yard, London W1.
01-734 7991.

Muir, Donna (105,107),
4th Floor, 44 Earlham Street,
London WC2.

Mynott, Lawrence (73,74),
20 Evelyn Gardens, London SW7.
01-584 5020 ext. 218.

Newton, Martin (56),
1st Mildreds Place, Canterbury,
Kent CT1 3SR.

Noome, Mike (247),
Andrew Archer Associates,
10 Glentworth Street,
London NW1. 01-487 3425.

Norrington, Bob (259),
44 Earlham Street, London WC2.
01-836 0919.

O'Keefe, Kevin M. D. (216,217),
6 Elfindale Road, Herne Hill,
London SE24 9NW. 01-274 2093.

P

Page, Rob (292), 76 Field Lane,
Teddington, Middlesex.
01-977 5036.

Pascoe, Terry (280),
c/o David Lewis Management,
52 Shaftesbury Avenue,
London W1V 1DE.

Penney, David (104,184),
19 Charlotte Street, London W1.
01-636 5901.

Pickard, Steve (32,33),
28c Kings Road, Richmond, Surrey.
01-948 4080.

Pollock, Ian (83,84,85,86,118,127),
7 Grove Terrace, Highgate Road,
London NW5. 01-485 6505.

Powell, Jenny (22,23,196),
53 Glebe Road, London SW13.
01-876 5114.

Prosser, Bill (111), 13 Avon Close,
Bradford-on-Avon, Wilts.
02216 6017.

Randell, Tony (141),
129 Upton Lane,
Forest Gate, London E7.
01-471 8656.

Rayner, Mary (205),
40 Halford Road, Richmond, Surrey.
01-940 3009.

Richardson, Peter (167),
31 Cambanks, Union Lane,
Cambridge. 0223 63825.

Roberts, Tony (180),
c/o Young Artists,
25 St. Pancras Way, London NW1.
01-387 2516.

Robins, Arthur Warrens (2,3,4,133,
134), Woodland Avenue, Cranleigh,
Surrey. 048-664 251.

Roche, Christine (62,63),
7 Archibald Road, London N7.
01-607 4728.

Roe, David (234),
c/o Transworld Publishers Ltd.,
Century House,
61/63 Uxbridge Road,
London W5 5SA. 01-579 2652.

Rose, Gerald (220), 'Ballards Shaw',
62 Sittingbourne Road, Maidstone,
Kent. Maidstone 52390.

Rowe, Eric (209),
c/o Transworld Publishers Ltd.,
Century House,
61/63 Uxbridge Road,
London W5 5SA. 01-579 2652.

Russell, George (255), Rolls Road,
London SE1. 01-237 0692.

Rylands, Ljiljana (250),
76a Belsize Park Gardens,
London NW3 4NG. 01-586 0878.

Sage, Angie (245), The Willows,
Riverside, Bourne End,
Buckinghamshire. 06285 23085.

Sanders, Brian (75,80,212,261),
c/o Artist Partners Ltd.,
14/18 Ham Yard, London W1.
01-734 7991.

Sanderson, Bill (92,93),
9 Ingram Street, Huntingdon,
Cambridgeshire. 0480 51904.

Sandford, Ron (201), 34 King Street,
Covent Garden, London WC2.

Sharrock, Christopher (117),
58 Huskisson Street,
Liverpool L8 7LR. 051-709 3690.

Sim, David (219),
c/o Royal College of Art,
Department of Illustration,
Exhibition Road, London SW4.
01-584 5020.

Simmonds, Posy (99),
4a Orde Hall Street, London WC1.
01-242 8929.

Sleight, Katy (137,138,139),
'Chegworth', Goring Road,
Steyning, Sussex BN4 3GF.

Smith, David Farwell (53),
94 Vallance Road,
London N22 4UG. 01-888 5557.

Smith, George (221),
c/o Young Artists,
25 St. Pancras Way, London NW1.
01-387 2516.

Smith, Graham (186),
2 Ackmar Road, Parsons Green,
Fulham, London SW6. 01-731 3094.

Smith, Ray (200),
c/o Jonathan Cape Ltd.,
30 Bedford Square, London WC1.
01-636 5764.

Southward, Ann (242),
5 Hillcrest Avenue, Whitehaven,
Cumbria.

Sowter, Nita (199), 18 Albert Street.
Cambridge. Cambridge 60062.

Steadman, Ralph (31,67),
113 New Kings Road, London SW6.
01-731 2089.

Stemp, Eric (222),
96 Hamilton Terrace, London NW8.
01-286 0291.

Stern, Simon (129,218),
19 Corringham Road,
London NW11. 01-458 8250.

Tenney, Eric (264),
80 Poplar Crescent, West Ewell,
Epsom, Surrey. 01-397 3362.

Terry, Mike (1,43), 10 Gate Street,
Lincoln's Inn Fields. London WC2.
01-402 1118.

Till, Peter (59,61,128,283),
42 Berkeley Road, London N8.
01-348 7736.

Thirsk, John (244), 15 Queen Street,
Stotford, Hitchin,
Hertfordshire SG5 4NX.
0462 731399.

Thompson, Graham (13),
23 The Poplars, St. Albans, Herts.

Thompson, John,
John Thompson Associates,
33 Eyre Street, London EC1R 5ET.
01-278 8568.

Thompson, Ken (7,8,48,159),
c/o Chris Meiklejohn,
31 King Street, Covent Garden,
London WC2.

Thompson, Nicholas John (14,30),
84 Dumbreck Road, Glasgow.

Thompson-Steinkrauss, John (161),
c/o John Martin & Artists Ltd.,
5 Wardour Street,
London W1V 3HE.

Trevithick, Mike (276),
32 Warner Road, London N8 7HD.
01-340 0832.

Vieweg, Cecil (50,51,163,164,165),
10 Clive Road, Twickenham,
Middlesex. 01-892 5877.

Voce, Louise (126,206),
9 College Road North, Crosby,
Liverpool L23 8UP. 051-924 4633.

Warner, Peter (160),
Boundary View, Hillside Road,
Tatsfield, Westerham, Kent.
095-98 270.

Weaver, Norman (102),
Lob's Cottage, Cromwell Road,
Worcester Park, Surrey. 01-337 1229.

White, Tim (231),
5 Grittleton Road, London W9.
01-286 5458.

Wijngaard, Juan (279),
c/o Spectron Artists Ltd.,
5 Dryden Street, London WC2.
01-240 2430.

Williams, Sylfia Ellen (177),
3 Rhes Ceiri,
Llanaelhaearn LL54 5AT, Gwynedd.
075 885 (LLithfaen) 693.

Winder, Ray (45),
R10 Gate Street, Lincolns Inn Fields,
London WC2. 01-402 1118.

Winn, Chris (198),
Littlewood House, Drayton,
Norwich, Norfolk. 0603 867519.

Woodcock, John (263),
56 Dulwich Road, Herne Hill,
London SE24. 01-274 7983.

Wright, Paul (169,170),
c/o John Martin and Artists Ltd.,
5 Wardour Street, London W1.
01-734 9000.

Wright, Terry (16),
27 Floral Street, London WC2.
01-836 3400.

Wurr, Penelope Jane (152,229),
1 Pikes End, Eastcote High Road,
Pinner, Middlesex. 01-866 8657.

Folio

Illustrators' & Designers' Agents
10 Gate Street
Lincoln's Inn Fields
London WC2

Telephone 01 242 9562/3
Telecopier 242 9564

With compliments

Artist Partners Limited
represent the following illustrators :

Adams Stephen	Dawson-Thomson Bill	Keane Gary	Rush Ken
Barrett Peter	Dell'Orco Pino	Knight David	Sanders Brian
Baylis and Adam	Froud Brian	Landels Angela	Sharp George
Beaven Howard	Garrett Jooce	Langdon David	Smilby
Binch Carol	Graham Tony	Lampitt Ronald	Soar Shirley
Bodek Stuart	Gilbert Yvonne	Lawrence John	Stemp Eric
Breeden Neil	Hants Harry	Lee Alan	Stymest Brian
Brittain Tom	Hargreaves Roger	Lindgren Goran	Tangye Howard
Cartwright Sue	Hartland Beryl	Littlewood Valerie	Tenney Eric
Chevins Hugh	Harker Douglas	Maxey Betty	Topolski Felix
Coombs Roy	Hills Gillian	Moyes Lizzie	Tweddell Kevin
Cooper Royston	Hunt Geoff	Raymond Charles	Vieweg Cecil
Cordery Don	Hutton Peter	Richards Tony	Weaver Norman
Crisp Stephen	Johnson Michael	Richens Keith	Western John
D'Achille Gino	Jones Gwyneth	Rix Aubrey	Withams Brian
Davies Claire	Jones Peter	Rose	Wynn Ken
Dalley Terence			

To help you make a choice the above illustrators specialize as follows :

Architecture and Landscape
Adams Stephen
Chevins Hugh
Dalley Terence
Jones Peter
Knight David
Lampitt Ronald
Sanders Brian
Western John

For Children and Decorative
Cartwright Sue
Cooper Royston
Froud Brian
Lee Alan
Littlewood Valerie
Maxey Betty

Richards Tony

Fashion
Hartland Beryl
Landels Angela
Rix Aubrey
Soar Shirley
Stemp Eric
Tangye Howard

Figurative and General
Beaven Howard
Breeden Neil
Binch Carol
Bodek Stuart
Chevins Hugh
Crisp|Stephen
D'Achille Gino

Davies Claire
Dawson-Thomson Bill
Dell'Orco Pino
Froud Brian
Garrett Jooce
Gilbert Yvonne
Hants Harry
Hills Gillian
Hutton Peter
Jones Gwyneth
Jones Peter
Johnson Michael
Keane Gary
Landels Angela
Lee Alan
Littlewood Valerie
Lofthouse Barbara
Maxey Betty
Moyes Lizzie

Raymond Charles
Richens Keith
Rix Aubrey
Sanders Brian
Sharp George
Stymest Brian
Tweddell Kevin
Topolski Felix
Vieweg Cecil
Wynn Ken

Humour
Hargreaves Roger
Lindgren Goren
Langdon David
Smilby

Industrial, Marine and Aviation
Brittain Tom
Chevins Hugh
Coombs Roy
Harker Douglas
Hunt Geoff
Hutton Peter
Rush Ken
Tweddell Kevin
Withams Brian

Scraperboard
Lawrence John
Rose

Still Life and Natural History
Adams Stephen
Barrett Peter

Brittain Tom
Cartwright Sue
Coombs Roy
Cordery Don
Dawson-Thomson Bill
Garrett Jooce
Graham Tony
Harker Douglas
Moyes Lizzie
Raymond Charles
Richards Tony
Sanders Brian
Tenney Eric
Weaver Norman

Visualising and Storyboards
Sharp George
Hants Harry
Richens Keith

14-18 Ham Yard, Gt. Windmill Street, London W1V 8DE. Telephone No: 01-734-7991.

LONDON:
IAN FLEMING AND ASSOC. LTD.
3 CARLISLE STREET, LONDON W1V 5RH
TEL: 01-734 6196/439 3400
TELECOPIER: 01-439 3400

NEW YORK
McCATHERN McKINNLY
2 PARK AVENUE, NEW YORK 10016
TEL: 212-889 3533

ANN MEISEL

GRAHAM BERRY

ADRIAN CHESTERMAN

TOM STIMPSON

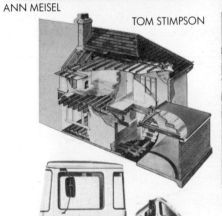

JOHN FARMAN

PETER HOLT

PAUL HIGGENS

PETER BENTLEY

JOHN BUTLER

DANNY KLEINMAN

MIKE BELL

Have you ever wished you were better informed?

Next time you see an impressive piece of illustration
and wonder who was responsible, try giving us a ring.

Young Artists Representing

Colin Backhouse
Maureen Booth
Jim Burns
Richard Clifton-Dey
Chris Collingwood
Gordon Crabb
Alan Daniels
Graham Dean

Les Edwards
Bob Fowke
Linda Garland
Roger Garland
Peter Goodfellow
Terry Hadler
Marc Harrison
Colin Hay

Philip Hood
Stuart Hughes
Susan Hunter
Bob Layzell
David Leeming
Angus McKie
John Miller
Terry Oakes

Nancy Petley-Jones
Tony Roberts
George Smith
Brian Sweet
Peter Tybus
Adrian Wright
and Bob Marchant
(Photography)

Young Artists: 25, St. Pancras Way, London, NW1 0PX Telephone: 01-387 2516/7

Detail of an illustration by Richard Clifton-Dey, commissioned for an original advertising concept by Roger Stanier for THE TIMES.

WE'LL SHOW FRENCH GOLD, B.B.D.O. AND COLLETS YOUR SPECIES BEFORE YOU WILL.

Wouldn't you love a rep who was always in the right places at the right time?

Well, right now the Creative Handbook seems to be the hottest rep in the advertising world.

There is simply no better way you, as creative suppliers, can show your work, or put across your facilities, to over 2,600 art and print buyers and the key decision makers who buy creative services.

This year more than 4,000 copies have been distributed among the top creative people in leading London and provincial advertising agencies and major national advertisers, and will be used by double this number.

A recent survey disclosed that 87% turned to it for new or alternative suppliers. Others used it as a portfolio reference, a telephone directory, or a source of new business leads.

The Creative Handbook covers just about every creative service. So before you heave your portfolio up numerous flights of stairs, contact Annie Roe or Stewart Swindell at: The Creative Handbook Ltd., 9 Chichester Chambers, 13 Chichester Rents, Chancery Lane, London WC2. Tel: 01-405 2663/4/5.

They'll tell you how to be represented in the Creative Handbook. Then, with a bit of luck, you won't have to call French Gold, BBDO, Collets and the like.

They'll call you.

Photo: Peter Baylis

THE CREATIVE HANDBOOK.

After David Abbott, Tim Delaney, Neil Godfrey and John Webster have thumbed through your work, how can you show it to anyone else?

Send it to Crisp Lamination first.
36 Maiden Lane, London WC2. 01-240 5299.

THE SUNDAY TIMES COLOUR MAGAZINE—Trimmed size 9⅝″ × 11¹¹⁄₁₆″ 245mm. × 300mm.

PAGE   10/12 PLANTIN

ART		
COPY		
FASHION/FEATURE		
EDITOR		
PRODUCTION		
LAWYER		

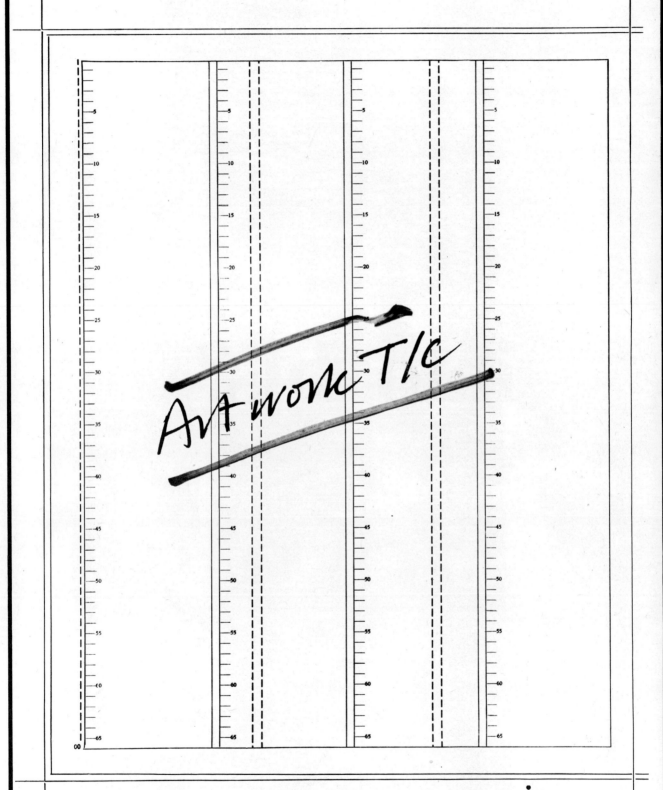

Can you turn this

```
S P A C E
```

into this?

COLIN ANDREW

JOE PETAGNO

BOB MARTIN

DAVID MCALLISTER

TIM WHITE

TONY MASERO

TIME DESIGN ASSOCIATES

5 BIRCH TERRACE, HANLEY, STOKE-ON-TRENT, ST1 3JN. telephone 0782 20544

The Allegro 1750 Sport

In addition to our illustration work we also produce: Design, typography,
headline and text photosetting, mechanicals, black and white retouching, presentation material,
photoprinting, lettering and silk screen printing–all beautifully and through 24 hours.

THE ARTSHOP GROUP.
57 North Wharf Road, London W2 1LA. 01-402 9161. Telecopier 01-402 9160 & 9168.

Which is the Normacolor Art Marker?

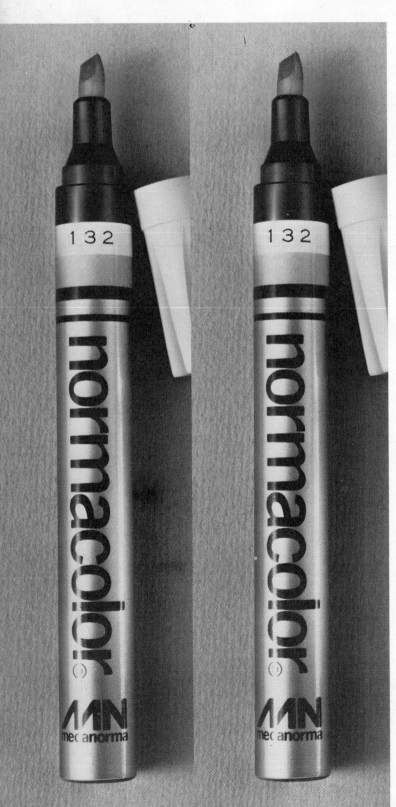

Normacolor Art Markers are brought to you by Mecanorma, a company with a total commitment to quality control which borders on fanaticism.

The right-hand Art Marker of the two illustrated is a case in point.

Like its fellow marker (which was approved for distribution) it has a writing life of between 1,412 and 1,462 metres.

Its colour is one of those in the 92-colour Mecanorma Art Marker range. And it matches the colour of its companion marker perfectly. Just as it matches the colour shown against its reference number in the hand-prepared Mecanorma Swatch Book which costs a mere 25p. (Mecanorma maintain that hand-preparation is the *only* way to achieve true colour fidelity. How fussy can you get?)

Its tip is of compressed polyester fibre which will keep its shape and not spread throughout its useful life.

Its cap is a nice snug, air-tight fit and the reference number corresponds to that on the barrel and the Swatch Book.

Its barrel is pencil-shaped for ease of handling. But on close examination, it was found to have a minute flaw in the seal moulding near the tip. (The inquest as to *why,* is probably still going on). Mecanorma feared that, as a result, the Marker, unlike all other Mecanorma Art Markers, could not be left uncapped for 24 hours, recapped for 48 hours and then used again with no loss of marking power or life.

So it was rejected.

'Tut-tut' you may say. Yes, but Mecanorma spotted the trouble before you had a chance to. What's more, they apply the same vigilance to every product in the Normacolor range—the 172 different coloured films in matt and glossy versions, the 170 different coloured papers and the remarkable and modestly priced swatch books.

They do so in order that every one of the thousands of Mecanorma products on sale *is* a Mecanorma product. And no question about it.

The Normacolor System.

Mecanorma Limited, 49/51 Central Street, London EC1V 8AB.
Telephone: 01-253 1102/1103, 01-253 1427, 01-253 0261.
Telex: 22623.

CARTER MATAINE SOUTHERN LIMITED, TUNBRIDGE WELLS

Nine of the most professional illustrators around are represented by Michele Beint

Alan Austin · David Draper · Peter Ferris
Victor Herbert · John Holder · Gray Jolliffe
Allan Manham · Dan Pearce · Elly Robinson

Beint & Beint · 2 Elms Road · London SW4 · 01-720 2087

As Agents—they're more than just a list of Artists!!

Linden Artists Ltd

86 PETTY FRANCE, ST. JAMES'S, LONDON SW1H 9EA
Telephone: 01·222 3050 01·222 4065/6

Among the entries selected for this year's Exhibition and reproduced in this annual are plates from 'FAERIES', a multi-colour sketchbook tracing the history of Faerie.

The artists, Alan Lee and Brian Froud, have collaborated closely in the aim of offering a unique visual journey through the realm of Faerie, thus this book will be of special interest to all lovers of illustration.

Brian Froud has already been strongly established in Britain with Pan's edition of 'The Land of Froud'.

Soon to be published by Harry N Abrams (USA) and Souvenir Press in hardcover and by Bantam (USA) and Pan. Edited and designed by David Larkin.

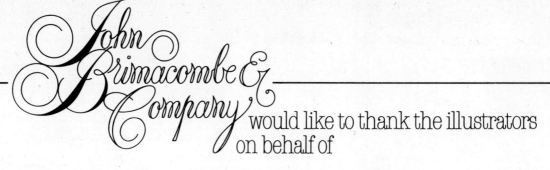

Our numbers in the book.

Colin Barnes
Tony Coles
Hugh Dixon
Susan Edwards
Klim Forster
John Geary/64
Donald Gott
Lynda Gray/69, 256
Jene Hawkins
David Hughes
Roy Knipe/38
Frank Langford
Carol Lawson/176, 278
Chris Molan
Chris Moore/12, 142, 210
Sue Porter
Jenny Powell/22, 23, 196
Angie Sage/245
Paul Slater
Petula Stone
Juan Wijngaard/279

The numbers listed refer to illustrations in this annual.
Specimen sheets of all our artists' work are available.

Call Ken Kirkland or Martin Borland

01-240 2430

SPECTRON ARTISTS LTD
5 Dryden Street, London WC2E 9NW
or via The Art Box, Amsterdam
or Artwork SA, Brussels

CORGI

1979

A WEALTH

OF

BESTSELLERS

CORGI BOOKS ARE A DIVISION OF TRANSWORLD PUBLISHERS LTD.,
CENTURY HOUSE, 61-63 UXBRIDGE ROAD, LONDON W5 5SA, ENGLAND

If you're looking for one of London's top illustrators, try your A-Z.

Behind each of these illustrations there's a folio full of five star work. If you'd like to see a particular artist's work, or a representative selection of all our artists' work, give us a ring. Alternatively, pop in and browse through the books with a glass of wine. You'll find us at 48 Grafton Way, London W.1. If you're not sure where that is, look it up in your A-Z.

580-5405. 387-6115/6
Telecopier 388-3607

ALL TYPES OF ILLUSTRATION FOR ALL TYPES OF ART DIRECTOR